D1077913

Scottish Christian Names

LESLIE ALAN DUNKLING

Scottish Christian Names

AN A-Z OF FIRST NAMES

JOHNSTON AND BACON

LONDON AND EDINBURGH

A Johnston & Bacon book published by
Cassell Ltd.
35 Red Lion Square, London WC1R 4SG
and Tanfield House, Tanfield Lane, Edinburgh EH3 5LL
and at Sydney, Auckland, Toronto, Johannesburg,
an affiliate of
Macmillan Publishing Co., Inc.,
New York

© Leslie Alan Dunkling, 1978

All rights reserved. No part of this publication may be reproduced,
stored in any retrieval system, or transmitted, in any form or by any
means, electronic, mechanical, photocopying, recording or otherwise,
without the prior permission in writing of the Publishers.

First published 1978

ISBN 0 7179 4249 X

Printed in Great Britain by
Lowe & Brydone Printers Limited, Thetford, Norfolk 977

CONTENTS

Acknowledgements vi
Introduction 1
SCOTTISH CHRISTIAN NAMES 9
Select Bibliography 139
Index 143

ACKNOWLEDGEMENTS

The following have helped to make the compiling of this book an easier and more pleasant task, and I gladly acknowledge their help: Miss Margaret Kerrigan of Kilmarnock, Mrs Joan Stewart of Leacklee, Miss Kate Maguire of Glasgow, Hamish Norbrook of Aberdeen, Mrs Jenny Carter of Edinburgh, Mrs Elisabeth Inglis of Edinburgh, Willie McRobert of Ayr, F. K. Macdonald of Peterculter, Reginald Dunkling of Huntly. I also owe a considerable debt of gratitude to various members of staff in the offices of the Scottish Registrar General, Edinburgh.

Members of The Names Society will notice in many of the entries that comments they have made have borne fruit. I am particularly in debt to them for many of the name quotations. The one at the beginning of this book, for instance, was brought to my attention by Stephen York.

For basic statistical research, especially that which in this book has allowed me to comment on name usage in England and Wales, I am once again indebted to my colleague C. V. Appleton.

Finally, for specific and helpful comments made at type-script and proof stage I am most grateful to William Gosling, Professor James S. McEwan, and the Reverend William Matheson.

LESLIE ALAN DUNKLING
Lady Day, 1978

What a wonderful thing to have a kid of one's own . . . don't afflict the poor little brat with a Celtic sort of name that nobody knows how to spell. She'll probably grow up psychic or something. People always grow up like their names. It took me thirty years to work off the effects of being called Eric. *If I wanted a girl to grow up beautiful I'd call her* Elizabeth, *and if I wanted her to be honest and a good cook I'd choose something like* Mary *or* Jane!

Part of a letter from George Orwell (but signed 'Eric') to Rayner Heppenstall, 16 April, 1940. From *Collected Essays, Journalism and Letters of George Orwell,* volume 2, published by Penguin.

INTRODUCTION

Scottish Christian names are to a large extent the same Christian names that are found throughout the English-speaking world and, for that matter, in all Christian countries. Nevertheless, the names used in Scotland have certain distinctive characteristics which reflect the history and nature of the country. There is the basic layer of Gaelic names, for example. There are the classical names such as **Aeneas, Hector** and **Hercules** which were introduced as 'substitutes' for Gaelic and Norse names at a time when the latter were unacceptable to the authorities. There is the frequent occurrence of famous clan names and surnames, pressed into use as Christian names. There is the adaptation of male names to female use by adding -ina or -ena to **Thomas, Peter, Jacob,** and the like. There is the fondness for French names which reflects the Auld Alliance. All these characteristics will emerge strongly in the pages that follow.

Even the 'shared' names, found in slightly modified form in most Christian countries, have often been made Scottish by the extent to which they have been used in Scotland, by the use of particular pet forms, and by their use in Scottish literature. I have tried to comment on all such matters throughout this book.

I have been especially concerned to give detailed notes about how each name has been used in Scotland during the last hundred years or so. Christian names have different kinds of meaning: etymological, historical and social. The traditional approach to Christian names has always, in my view, paid too little attention to the last of these. It is all very well to say that **Agnes**, for example, means 'chaste' and that from a historical point of view it is a fine old Scottish name. Both statements are true, but one can nevertheless understand why fewer and fewer Scottish parents use it each year as a first name. The name's 'social meaning' is no longer a particularly good one, though it becomes immediately better in some mysterious way if the old pronunciation *Anyes* or *Annis* is used. A name's social meaning is largely defined by the way it has been used within living memory—hence my detailed notes on that subject.

Christian names have yet another meaning, one which is highly subjective and personal. There are those who like old, familiar names, who will shrink from new arrivals, imported from the U.S.A. by means of films and television. And there are many who value newness and novelty for its own sake, who see no point in trying to preserve the past, and who are determined to use names which reflect the spirit of the age they live in.

I have tried to keep my views on this matter to myself. My aim has been to describe Scottish Christian names and their use, not prescribe. As it happens, I usually find that *every* name is interesting, either from a linguistic, historical or sociological point of view, or perhaps from all three. It is certainly necessary to bear all three in mind. To deal with Christian names from the specialised view of the linguist on the one hand, or the Scottish historian on the other, would seriously interfere with objectivity.

In my last book about Christian names, *First Names First* (Dent 1977), I was concerned to some extent with the psychology of names—how adults should assess their own names and make the best of them, as it were. In this book I am far more concerned with trying to provide young Scottish parents who are trying to find a name for a new member of the family with the information they need.

Parents might also like to bear the following points in mind
as they weigh up the advantages and disadvantages of each
name:

Spelling   Names which everyone can spell are useful. It
is surprising how many names have alternative spellings. If
you call your daughter **Catherine** expect to see her name
written as *Kathryn, Katharine,* etc., by relatives and
teachers. Exotic spellings (**Kristoffer, Margarette**) are
not a good idea.

Sexual ambiguity   Names which make the sex of the child
clear are to be preferred to those (e.g. **Leslie, Lindsay**)
which do not.

Form of name   Even if you intend to use the pet form of
a name (e.g. **Maggie**) in ordinary speech, it is best to give
the name in its formal version (**Margaret**). The child may
well need the more dignified form in later life.

Diminutives   You may intend to use the name in its
correct form at all times. It is nevertheless well to be aware
of the name's diminutive forms and decide whether they
are acceptable. Your child's friends will use them even if
you do not.

Nicknames   Beware of names that are temptingly close to
other words (**Dustin**—dustbin). Other children will quickly
seize upon the opportunity to make fun of the name-bearers.

Simplicity   A fairly simple, plain Christian name is
probably a good idea if you have an uncommon or long
surname. A common surname might be better 'balanced'
with a more elaborate Christian name.

Modishness   It is important to know whether a name is
fashionable or not when you give it to your child. A name
that is highly fashionable at any one moment (especially
a girls' name) is all too likely to become equally unfashionable in the future, thereby dating its bearer.
Names which have been out of fashion for over sixty years
generally become safe to bring back into use.

Popularity   Another problem connected with a name's
being very much in fashion is that several other children

in the class are likely to bear it. Your child may suffer the
indignity of having a number name tagged on at school,
and teachers have even been known to rename a child for
school purposes.

Tradition Established names often have an advantage
over 'new' names, which people may not know how to
spell, pronounce, etc.

Initials Christian names that make up a meaningful set
of initials with your surname should be carefully thought
about. Such initial words, or acronyms, often lead to nicknames.

Sound Beware of unfortunate sound combinations with
your surname (e.g. **Iris Tugh**).

Pronunciation Is there any doubt about how the name
you have in mind is pronounced? There are many names
which would be pronounced differently by different
speakers (e.g. **Charmian, Marcia, Irene**).

Meaning The original meaning of a name is one of its
least important aspects in modern times, unless the meaning
is instantly apparent (e.g. **Joy, Patience**). The latter type
of name often leads to repetitive comments in later life
which your child may well find tiresome.

Unusualness Particular care must be taken in the
bestowing of an 'unusual' name. People who bear such
names often say that they are a disadvantage during child-
hood and adolescence but can become an advantage in later
professional life.

Maiden surname It is a markedly Scottish habit to use
the mother's maiden surname as a Christian name. Great
discretion should be used in making this kind of transfer.
A maiden surname can always be used as a middle name if
there is any doubt about how it will function as a first name.

Adapted names The old Scottish habit of adapting the
name of a male relation for a daughter, adding -ina or -ena,
is now dying out. Such names usually resulted from a wish
to keep a traditional family name alive when there was no
son who could do so. The resulting names, however, often

looked rather clumsy and were much criticised. If they are used at all today, it should perhaps be as middle names rather than first names.

Placenames Scottish placenames are used fairly regularly as Christian names. The habit perhaps derives from the custom in the Highlands of addressing lairds by the name of their property. Used with discretion this kind of name transfer can lead to a distinctively Scottish Christian name, but 'oddness' must be avoided at all costs.

Name patterns Another custom now falling into disuse is the former rigid pattern of naming the first son after the paternal grandfather, the first daughter after the maternal grandmother, and so on. Once again, middle names could well be used to preserve these family names.

Middle names Most children are now given one middle name as well as a first name, though middle names of any kind were rare in Scotland before 1800. There is no reason why a second or third middle name should not be used. Apart from preserving family names, as indicated above, the child is given more choice of names later in life.

I hope these notes do not make the task of choosing a name for a child seem unduly difficult and complex. There is no reason why this should be so. Searching for a name can be one of the added pleasures of becoming a parent, especially since a study of our Christian names heightens our awareness of the society in which we live. With that in mind I offer this book not only to young Scottish parents, but to all those who are interested in the Scots and Scotland, past and present.

NOTES ON SOURCES

In 1864 the Scottish Registrar General published in his Annual Report an article called 'Nomenclature in Scotland.' Listed in this article were the 50 most common surnames

in Scotland, as revealed by the Indices of the Registers for
the years 1855, 1856 and 1858. There were also tables
supplied showing the comparative use of Christian names
during the same three years by families named *Smith,
Macdonald, Brown, Robertson* and *Thomson.* This count,
based on a total of 7379 Christian names, is the basis of the
figures quoted throughout this book for 1858.

In 1937 Appendix VII of the Scottish Registrar General's
Report was again concerned with 'Nomenclature in Scotland.' Every name given to a child born in Scotland in
1935 had been counted, and lists of the 100 most
frequently used names for boys and girls were published.
Variant spellings of the same name were counted together
in this survey, as they had been in 1864. The Registrar
noted that 616 different boys' names were used in 1935,
together with 727 different girls' names. Since details of
only 200 names in all were given, it may be wondered how
often others were used. We are told that 324 boys and 354
girls received names that occurred only once that year, and
none of the missing names could have been very important
from a statistical point of view. In a later Report, for
instance, the Registrar General pointed out that the top 100
names accounted for 93.9% of the boys born in a single year,
and 82.8% of the girls.

This later Report related to 'Personal Names in Scotland,
1958.' More detailed in its published form than either of the
two previous ones, it was made still more valuable for
researchers by a subsequent document entitled 'Forenames
in Scotland: 1958 Birth Indexes.' This listed alphabetically
every Christian name given to a child born in Scotland in
1958, with the number of occurrences alongside. Spelling
variants were treated as separate names. Clearly there
could be no more authoritative basis for making comments
about usage than a document of this kind, which exists
in no other English-speaking country.

No further official counts of Scottish Christian names
have been published. My remarks throughout the book

about what has happened in Scotland since 1958 are based mainly on an unofficial count made in 1977 at the General Register Office in Edinburgh. This was carried out by Mrs Jenny Carter, and was concerned with the names used during 1975 by the *Campbells, Smiths* and *Macdonalds*. I have also made use of the figures produced by Mrs Elisabeth Inglis, extracted from birth announcements in the *Scotsman* during 1977 and published in that newspaper, together with those prepared by J. K. Macdonald from similar announcements in the *The Press and Journal*, Aberdeen. An article in the *Oban Times*, published early in 1978, gave details of the popular and 'more exotic' names that had occurred in the newspaper's birth announcements during 1977. This article has been cited several times.

These various reports and surveys provide a sound basis for making comments about the use of individual names in Scotland since 1858. For earlier periods I have relied upon such authorities as Dr George F. Black, whose *Surnames of Scotland* was published in 1946. Since many Scottish surnames derive from the Christian names that were in use in the Middle Ages, there is much to be learnt from such a work. I have referred also to articles such as 'The Old Gaelic System of Personal Names' and 'Early Highland Personal Names,' both by A. MacBain and published by the Gaelic Society of Inverness (1895, 1898).

At my request, my friend C. V. Appleton also made a study of the Christian names occurring in 1100 marriages which took place in the Edinburgh area from 1584-1700 (see *The Register of Marriages for the Parish of Edinburgh*, The Scottish Record Society, 1905). His count of names made it quite clear that during the sixteenth and seventeenth centuries a small number of Christian names accounted for a very large percentage of the population. The commonest boys' names in use at the time were **John, James, William, Robert, Thomas, Alexander, Andrew, George, David, Patrick, Richard, Walter,**

Edward, Malcolm, Adam, Archibald. The girls were mostly named **Margaret, Janet, Agnes, Marion, Isobel, Catherine, Bessie, Jean, Elspeth, Helen, Elizabeth, Christian, Mary, Euphemia, Beatrix, Barbara, Alison, Sarah. Giles** was clearly in frequent use, always as a girls' name.

Throughout this book I have often thought it of interest to indicate whether a particular name had been used in Scotland before or after a period of intense usage elsewhere in the English-speaking world. I have taken the facts about Christian name usage in England and Wales, the U.S.A., Canada and Australia from my *Guinness Book of Names* (1974) and *First Names First* (1977). Full details are given in those books about how the counts were made.

In compiling this book I have also referred to many dictionaries and discursive works about names. I list some of the more useful titles in the Bibliography for those who would like to investigate further.

There is an Index at the back of the book which serves as a cross-reference to pet forms, etc., mentioned under the main headings.

SCOTTISH CHRISTIAN NAMES

A

Abram (m)   Hebrew, 'high father.' The original name of **Abraham**, 'father of a multitude.' Many such Old Testament names were formerly common in Scotland, but the Registrar General, in his Report for 1937, commented that **Abner, Gideon, Ezekiel,** etc., 'have now almost fallen into disuse.' Abram became a common name in the Shetlands when Scottish ministers from the mainland refused to baptise children with the Scandinavian names traditionally in use. **Jacob, Jeremiah, Obadiah, Hosea** replaced **Erik, Sigurd, Hakon, Olaf,** etc., which were used for boys. The girls became **Hagar, Rhoda, Tamar, Jemima,** etc. Some Old Testament names are now decidedly fashionable in Scotland, as elsewhere in the English-speaking world. Details will be found under the individual entries.

Adair (m)   Better known as a Scottish surname, but occasionally used as a Christian name in Scotland. This takes it back to its original role, for there is evidence to suggest that it represents a former Scottish pronunciation of **Edgar.**

Adam (m)   This Hebrew name derives from a word meaning 'red earth,' but it was probably the redness that was more important in ancient times. Charlotte Yonge, in

her *History of Christian Names,* points out that another form
of the name, **Edom,** was given to Esau after he had
sold his birthright for a dish of *red* lentils. The land occupied
by his descendants was also called Edom because of the
red rocks found there.

The early popularity of Adam in Scotland is attested by
the many surnames that derive directly from it, or from
diminutives of the name such as **Addie, Addy, Adkin,
Atty, Edie.** The surnames include *Adam(s), Addie, Addy,
Addison, Adamson, Acheson, Atkinson, Aiken, Aitken, Atkin,
Atkins, Eadie, Edie, Edison, Macadam,* etc. By coincidence
Edom is also found as a Scottish surname, since Adam
was formerly pronounced that way in broad Scots.

Adam was the 46th most frequently bestowed boys' name
in Scotland in 1935. By 1958 it had dropped to 85th place
and it is now little used. It may well return to favour, having
been immensely successful in all other English-speaking
countries since the 1960's.

The Gaelic form of Adam is **Adhamh,** dialectal **Adaidh.**
The latter gave rise to further surnames such as *Macadie,
Macaddie, Maccaddie,* 'son of Adam,' and led to the Scots
diminutive, **Yiddie.**

Adamina (f) This is said to have been an eighteenth-
century Scottish invention, a feminine form of **Adam**. A
recent Dutch dictionary of Christian names (*Woordenboek
van Voornamen,* 1976) shows it to be in use in the Nether-
lands. It also occurs in countries such as Bulgaria and
Poland, but no trace of it appears in recent Scottish sources.

Adamnan (m) The name of the biographer of St
Columba, generally taken to mean 'little **Adam**.' The
Gaelic form of the name, **Adhamhnan,** is pronounced
Yownan.

Adrian (m) Latin, 'one from Adria,' a city in Northern
Italy. The name of this city, formerly a port on the Adriatic

Sea, probably derives from Illyrian *adur*, 'water, sea,' as Adrian Room explains *(Place Names of the World)*. The Latin form of the personal name was **Hadrianus.** It was borne by the Roman emperor responsible for building **Hadrian's** wall. Adrian has been quietly used in Scotland. Since 1965, however, it has been decidedly fashionable in England and Wales, and Scottish usage may well increase in the 1980's. The French feminine form **Adrienne** is preferred in Scotland to the Latin **Adriana.**

Aed, Aedh (m)   A Gaelic name meaning 'fire'. The Latin form is **Aidus,** best known in its diminutive form, **Aidan.** The later Gaelic spelling was **Aodh,** and this was sometimes equated with **Odo** in Latin documents. **Hugh** or **Hugo** was the English name more usually substituted for it, however. The surnames *Mackay, Mackie, Maccay*, etc., mean 'son of Aodh.'

Aeneas (m)   A Greek name meaning 'praiseworthy.' Its use in Scotland (and Ireland) has mostly been due to its accidental similarity to **Aonghas,** anglicised as **Angus,** rather than admiration for the Trojan hero whose exploits were celebrated by Virgil and others. (Compare the use of **Hector** as a substitute for **Eachann.**) The spelling **Eneas** is often found.

Africa (f)   Gaelic **Oighrig** or **Eithrig.** This hardly looks like a Scottish Christian name, but it was popular as such in the twelfth century and continued in general use until as late as the eighteenth century. It occurred in a variety of forms, including **Affrica, Afreka, Affreka, Eafric, Effric, Effrick.** Shortened to **Effie,** it then tended to become confused with **Euphemia.**

Needless to say, the Scottish Christian name had nothing to do with the name of the continent (which is thought to derive from an Arabic word *afira,* 'to be dusty'). The Christian name looked back to a Celtic original of unknown

meaning, though some scholars have linked it to the name
of a river goddess—also seen, it is claimed, in the name of
the River Affric. Johnston *(Place-Names of Scotland)*
repeats Dr M'Bain's suggestion that the source was Gaelic
ath-breac, 'somewhat speckled,' and this is followed by
Black *(Surnames of Scotland)*. A different explanation of
the name is offered by Woulfe *(Irish Names for Children)*.
He cites the forms **Aifric, Aifrice, Afric, Africa** and
Aphria, referring all of them to a Celtic word meaning
'pleasant.' Kneen *(The Personal Names of the Isle of Man)*
testifies to the popularity of **Affrica, Aurick, Averick,**
etc., from the twelfth century onwards, but offers no
etymology. See also **Erica, Euphemia.**

Agnes (f) The Latin form of a Greek name meaning
'chaste,' but a Scottish name by adoption. It has been
especially Scottish in the twentieth century. Use of the
name has drastically declined since 1900 in every English-
speaking country, but Scottish parents remained faithful
to it until very recent times. In 1958, for example, 557
girls born in Scotland received the name, which means that
an Agnes born that year is fifty times more likely to be
Scottish than English, American, Canadian or Australian.
However, Agnes was only the 22nd most frequently used
name in Scotland in 1958, whereas it was 7th in 1935 and
8th in 1858. The most recent count (1975) shows that the
name is being less and less used by young Scottish
parents.

As the name of one of the most popular saints, Agnes
enjoyed international favour for centuries. In Scotland the
name was also associated from the fourteenth century
onwards with the Countess of March, known as 'Black
Agnes.' Scott, in *Tales of a Grandfather* (1827-9), explains
the nickname of this 'Brawling, boistr'rous Scottish wench'
by referring to her dark complexion. Others (e.g. Brewer)
say that she earned her name 'through the terror of her

deeds.' All agree that she made a spirited defence of Dunbar against the English.

The name's intensive usage in Scotland has led to many diminutive forms, including **Aggie, Aggy, Nessa, Nessie, Nesta,** which are occasionally given as independent names. Perhaps the most extraordinary compliment to the name has been the use in Scotland of its reversed form, **Senga,** which is still to be found. A correspondent, Mrs Joan Stewart, also reports from the Western Isles on the use there of **Agnesina.**

Aidan (m) A diminutive of the once popular Gaelic name **Aed** and the name of a popular saint. It is in occasional use.

Aileen (f) See **Eileen.**

Ailsa (f) Used for over a century as a Christian name, though almost exclusively in Scotland. There are now signs of interest being shown in the name elsewhere in the English-speaking world. Some writers (e.g. Partridge, Johnson and Sleigh) have linked it with **Elsa,** a name which has never been particularly popular in Scotland. It is far more likely to be a direct borrowing from Ailsa Craig. In *Pseudonyms,* by J. F. Clarke, Ellen Terry is quoted as saying: 'Ailsa Craig! What a magnificent name for an actress!'

Ainslie (m, f) This surname probably derives from the English placename Annesley, the origin of which is obscure. It has been used in Scotland to name both boys and girls. The spelling **Aynslie** also occurs.

Alan (m) The favourite modern spelling in Scotland of a name also found as **Allan** or **Allen,** forms which are probably transferred from the surnames. Usage in Scotland for boys born in 1958: Alan, 1136; Allan, 481; Allen, 14.

The French **Alain** was also used twice. Allan was the nineteenth-century preference. The Gaelic form of the name is **Ailean,** or **Ailin** in Ireland. Black *(Surnames of Scotland)* suggests a derivation from *ail,* 'rock,' but various other explanations have been suggested by scholars. Alan (a coincidently similar name) was a favourite amongst the Bretons, who introduced it to England in the eleventh century at the time of the Norman Conquest. All that can be said for certain is that the name is ancient and Celtic. Its early popularity in Scotland led to its becoming a surname in various forms, e.g. *Callan, Callen, MacAllan, MacAllen,* etc. The name has been as popular in Scotland in the late 1970's as it ever was.

Alana (f) A feminine form of **Alan** used by Scottish parents. It sometimes appears as **Allana.** Ronan Coghlan *(Irish Christian Names)* connects the occasional Irish use of this name with the expression *a leanbh,* 'O child.'

Alasdair (m) The 'correct' Gaelic form of **Alexander,** more often spelt **Alistair** or **Alastair** in modern times because of its pronunciation. Other spellings used by Scottish parents in recent years include **Alaister, Alaster, Alistar, Alister, Allistair, Allister.** Scott has a minstrel called **Allaster** in *Rob Roy* (1817). Alasdair was in 82nd place in the 1958 Scottish popularity table, with Alastair in 48th place and Alistair in 37th place. If the spelling variations are disregarded, on the grounds that parents were basically choosing the same name, then the combined totals would easily have made it one of the top twenty names. The name remains primarily Scottish, though it has recently begun to be used in other English-speaking countries.

Albert (m) A Germanic name meaning 'noble bright.' It was used in late Victorian times in Britain, presumably because of Prince Albert. It was the 40th most frequently used name for boys born in Scotland in 1935, but it had fallen to 77th place in 1958. It is now completely out of fashion. The normal pet forms are **Al** or **Bert.**

Alberta, Albertina (f) These are feminine forms of **Albert** which have occasionally been used in Scotland. The Canadian province Alberta was named in honour of Princess Louise Caroline Alberta, wife of the former Governor-General, the Marquis of Lorne.

Alexander (m) Originally a Greek name, usually explained as 'defender of men,' though Robert Graves in *Greek Myths* suggests 'he who wards off men.' Alexander became a royal name in Scotland in the twelfth century when Alexander I came to the throne. Alexander's mother, Queen Margaret, had been brought up in the Hungarian Court, where the name would have been familiar. Alexander II and III subsequently ruled in Scotland for most of the thirteenth century, thoroughly establishing the name.

In 1858 Alexander was the 4th most frequently used name for Scottish boys. It was still in 5th position in 1935, and in 7th position in 1958. By that time several Gaelic forms of the name, especially **Alistair, Alastair** and **Alasdair,** were also in use. Diminutive forms such as **Alec, Aleck, Alex, Alick, Allie, Ally, Andy, Sander, Saunder** and **Sandy** have all been used as independent names. It was Sandy which led in former times to the general nickname for a Scotsman, namely 'Sawney' or 'Sawny'. Lowland pronunciation of the name in the nineteenth century was *Elshender* or *Elshie,* as indicated by Sir Walter Scott in *The Black Dwarf* (1816).

Alexandra (f) This feminine form of **Alexander** has now largely replaced **Alexandrina** in Scotland. Alexandra was in 69th position in the list of girls' names used in 1958. Other forms of the name used that year included **Alexa, Alexanderia, Alexanderina, Alexanderine, Alexandrea, Alexandrena, Alexandrine, Alexena,**

Alexina, Alexine. A Scottish pet form is **Lexie.** See also **Alexis** and **Sandra.** Woulfe *(Irish Names for Children)* mentions **Alastriona** and **Alastrina** as Gaelic feminine forms of Alexander, but these do not seem to have been used in Scotland.

Helena Swan *(Girls' Christian Names)* mentions that the ancient Greeks sometimes interchanged the names Alexandra and **Cassandra,** assuming them to be the same. One can hardly imagine two ladies more different, from an etymological point of view. Alexandra is 'she who wards off men;' Cassandra is 'she who entangles men.'

Alexandrina (f)   A feminine form of **Alexander** which was the 70th most frequently used name for girls in Scotland in 1935, but later it was replaced by **Alexandra.** In 1819 Queen Victoria was christened Alexandrina Victoria, her first name being in honour of her godfather, Alexander I of Russia.

Alexis (f)   In Scotland this name is now used exclusively for girls, and is thought of as a feminine form of **Alexander.** It began, however, as a boys' name, meaning 'helper.' It was the descriptive nickname in Greek of a saint whose real name is not known. The Russian **Aleksej (Alexei)** is the same name. The original feminine forms of Alexis were **Alexia** or **Alexa.** These are still occasionally used by Scottish parents, but they are thought of as feminines of Alexander.

Alice (f)   In 1605 William Camden *(Remains Concerning Britain)* correctly explained the origin of this name as 'abridged from **Adeliz.**' This in turn was a French version of the German **Adelheitis,** later **Adelheid. Adelaide** is the modern French form of the name, whose original elements combined to mean 'nobleness.'

Alice became in Latin **Alicia,** a form which is preferred by some Scottish parents. **Alys** was an early English spelling, and this too has been used in Scotland in recent times. Alice itself has been overtaken in Scotland by its own diminutive, **Alison.** Its former great popularity (Alice was the 24th most frequently used name for girls in Scotland in 1935), possibly owed much to a Scottish fondness for **Alexander.** Many parents must have seen Alice as a feminine form of **Alec** or **Alick.** It may also have been confused with **Elizabeth** through such pet forms as **Elsie** and **Elise.** Scottish pet forms of Alice include **Ailie, Allie, Ally** and **Ellie.**

A novel by Lord Lytton called *Alice* was published in 1838. One of his characters says: 'A sweet name, is it not? it accords so well with her (Alice's) simple character.' This book may have helped the name along, but it received its real boost in 1865 with the publication of *Alice in Wonderland.* This made the name a great favourite for the next thirty years.

Mrs Elisabeth Inglis, who records annually the names of children whose births are announced in the *Scotsman,* reports on the occasional use of **Ailidh** and **Ailis,** Gaelic forms of Alice and its diminutives.

Alison, Allison (f) Other forms of this name used in Scotland include **Allyson, Alyson, Alisoun, Alysoun. Alisanne** and **Alysanne,** both used by Scottish parents in 1958, seem to show a wish to identify the name with **Alice Anne.** Historically, however, the -on was a French dimunitive ending added to **Alis (Alice).** The name appeared in medieval English poems as Alisoun. Chaucer's girl of that name is said to be 'more pleasant to look on than a flowering pear tree.'

In 1935 Alice was used by Scottish parents three times as often as Alison. By 1958 Alison/Allison was used six times as often as Alice. The rise of Alison in Scotland was later followed by a spell of popularity in England and Wales, but the name remains distinctively Scottish. The *Oban Times* referred to it in an article about Christian

names (12 January 1978) as 'a new name on the West
Highland scene which was much used in 1977.' **Allie** and
Ally are pet forms.

Alpin, Alpine (m)   Gaelic **Ailpein.** The name of at least
two Pictish kings which survives mainly in surname form:
Macalpin, Macalpine, Elphin, etc. It is possibly related to
the Latin name **Albinus (Alban),** 'white'. The European
Alps may also derive their name from this source, though
Adrian Room *(Place Names of the World)* mentions the
Celtic word *alp*, 'rock, mountain.' St Patrick is referred to in
some Gaelic poems as a Macalpine.

Amanda (f)   A Latin name meaning 'lovable.' It has
been very popular in England and Wales since 1950, and
has recently been much used in Scotland.

Amy (f)   French *aimée*, 'loved.' Little used in modern
Scotland, but frequently found in former times, e.g., in
various clan histories. The name was also used as a pet
form of **Amabel.** Sir Walter Scott made the beautiful
Amy Robsart the heroine of his *Kenilworth* (1821). Amy
has been one of the most popular names in the U.S.A. in the
late 1970's, partly because of the publicity given to it by
President Carter's daughter.

Andrea (f)   The most popular modern feminine form of
Andrew, but its use is by no means confined to Scotland.
More Scottish, in terms of usage, are **Andrena, Andreana,
Andrene, Andrewina, Andrina, Andrine, Andriene,
Andrianna, Andreena, Andrean, Dreena** and **Rena.** All
these names were given to girls born in Scotland in 1958.

Andrew (m)   Originally a Greek name meaning 'manly.'
As the name of Scotland's patron saint, Andrew has
naturally long been popular. The Scottish Registrar
General's Report in 1858 showed it to be the 9th most

frequently given name for boys, a position it retained in 1935. It was still in 13th place in 1958, and a recent unofficial count (1975) indicates that it is currently one of the top ten names. It has been very much in fashion since the 1950's in almost every other English-speaking country.

The name's early association with Scotland is reflected in the frequency of Scottish surnames which are based on Andrew itself, or on diminutives such as **Andie, Andy, Dand, Dandie, Dandy.** These include *Anderson, Andrews, Andison, Drew, Gillanders, Macandrew,* etc.

'Dandy,' as applied to a silly, foppish man has traditionally been associated with Andrew, but 'one spoiled by overmuch dandling' is an alternative origin suggested by *Chamber's Twentieth Century Dictionary.*

The Latin form of Andrew, **Andreas,** is sometimes used in Scotland, as are the Gaelic versions, **Aindrea** and **Anndra.** Recently **Drew** has been especially popular as an independent name.

Angela (f)   A form of the word 'angel'. It was imported into Scotland in the early 1950's and quickly became one of the top fifty names (39th in 1958). Its use has been slowly declining in the late 1970's. Other variations of the name include **Angeline, Angie** and **Angelina.** The male form of the name, **Angelo,** was used to name three boys born in Scotland in 1958.

Angus (m)   Gaelic **Aonghas,** 'unique choice.' Formerly common in Ireland, but now associated almost exclusively with Scotland. The 61st most frequently used male name in 1958, according to the Scottish Registrar General's Report. **Aeneas (Eneas)** is traditionally used as a substitute for it, while *Macinnes, Mackinnes,* etc., 'son of Angus,' are amongst the surname forms.

Angusina (f)   A feminine form of **Angus** occasionally used in Scotland. It is usually pronounced *Angusēna.*

Ann, Anne (f)   English and French forms of the Hebrew name **Hannah,** which derives from a word meaning 'favour, grace.' **Annie** was the preferred form in the nineteenth century, and this still survives more vigorously in Scotland than in any other English-speaking country. The Latinised **Anna** has long been used by Scottish parents, and was ranked 68th in 1935. By 1958 it had lost ground considerably in Scotland. It may well stage a come-back, as it has become the fashionable replacement for Ann/Anne in England and North America in the 1970's. Hannah itself has also regained popularity since 1970, especially in England. The French diminutive **Annette** enjoyed a spell in the limelight during the 1950's throughout Britain, but this name has since tended to fade away. **Anita,** a Spanish diminutive of the name Ann/Anne, followed a similar pattern.

Usage of the various forms in Scotland in 1958 was as follows: Anne, 1300; Ann, 975; Annie, 187; Annette, 129; Anna, 92; Hannah, 28; Anita, 25.

Although a common name in its various forms throughout the Christian world, the recent tendency in English-speaking countries has been for Ann/Anne to be used as a middle name rather than a first name. It is easily the commonest feminine middle name in England, the U.S.A. and Canada. While it has never been a distinctively Scottish Christian name, it is likely to become so, if Scottish parents remain faithful to it.

Annabella (f)   Gaelic **Anabla,** also **Barabal,** perhaps through confusion with **Barbara.** A name well known in Scottish history as **Annabel** or Annabella. The mother of James I of Scotland, for example, was Annabel Drummond. The name has been consistently but quietly used by Scottish parents in the last hundred years, with **Annabelle** as a new variation. Former pronunciation of the name is indicated by **Annaple,** a name given by Scott to characters in *The Heart of Midlothian* (1818) and *The*

Black Dwarf (1816). Poe's *Annabel Lee* made the name known in North America, but it has not been frequently used there. As for its origin, it could simply have been an invention, meant to imply 'beautiful **Anna**,' or it could be a mistaken form of **Amabel,** 'lovable.'

Anthony (m)   From a Roman clan name, **Antonius,** of unknown origin. The spelling **Antony** is the correct one from a historical point of view, but in Scotland in 1958 Anthony was used by 282 parents, Antony by only 9. One problem with the *h*-spelling is that North American speakers tend to pronounce the name as written. Anthony was especially popular in Scotland from 1935-65, during which period **Tony** was also given as an independent name. The pet form **Nanty** is used by Sir Walter Scott in *Redgauntlet* (1824).

Antonia (f)   A feminine form of **Anthony/Antony** which has been increasingly used in Scotland in the late 1970's. **Toni** and **Tonia,** the pet forms, are also given as independent names.

Archibald (m)   Originally a Germanic name, composed of elements meaning 'excellent, noble, true' and 'bold.' However, -bald was assumed by Gaelic-speakers to be the word 'bald' = 'hairless,' which was the usual sign of a tonsured monk. Archibald was therefore used to translate the Gaelic name **Gilleasbuig (Gillespie),** where *gille* means '(shaven) servant or devotee.' The latter half of Gillespie means 'bishop,' and the Arch- of Archibald was possibly thought to connect with the first element of 'arch-bishop.' But if the name was adopted in Scotland— at first by the *Campbell* chiefs, much later by the country as a whole—for the wrong reasons, this did not prevent its becoming extremely popular. In 1858 it was the 13th most frequently used male name. It was in 20th place in 1935,

58th place in 1958. This made it a markedly Scottish name in terms of usage.

The English comedian, George Robey (1869-1954) had a great success with a song called *Archibald, Certainly Not,* which seems to have had a highly detrimental effect on the name's image. For some time writers, especially writers outside Scotland, have tended to use the name for characters who are meant to be upper-class idiots. The diminutive forms **Arch, Archie, Archy** and **Airchie** fortunately manage to steer clear of such associations. Scottish surnames such as *Baldie, Baldy, Baldison* may derive from 'descendant of Archibald,' though the Old English personal name **Baldwin,** 'bold friend,' may have been the origin of such names.

Arlene (f)   This is something of a mystery name, but one given to 53 Scottish girls in 1958 and no doubt to hundreds of others before and after that year. Several dictionaries list Arlene as a Celtic name meaning 'pledge.' This tradition was begun by *What Shall We Name The Baby?* (Winthrop Ames)—an influential American publication which first appeared in 1935. No doubt the compiler of this book linked the name with the word 'arle,' which occurs in the phrase 'arle-penny' or 'arles-penny.' 'Arles' meant 'money given in confirmation of a bargain, especially that given when engaging a servant.' In Scott's *Old Mortality* (1816) we find: 'Ye gae me nae arles, indeed.' However, there is no serious evidence of any kind that justifies the extension of this meaning to the name Arlene. It will probably never be possible to give an exact 'meaning' for Arlene. The name bears all the signs of being a blend of other names, or an arbitrary invention. Nevertheless, it has been fairly well used in the U.S.A., Canada and England, as well as in Scotland.

Arthur (m)   Gaelic **Artair.** As Scottish surnames like *Macarthur, Maccairter* and *Maccarter* indicate, Arthur was in early use in Scotland. First mention of it occurs in Adamnan's *Life of St Columba* (as **Arturius**), and this led many scholars to look for a Celtic origin. A suitable root would be *artos*, 'bear,' an element which also occurs in names like **Artgal** and **Artbran.** However, there are references in Roman writings to a *gens* (clan or sept) who bore the name **Artorius.** One of its members was the friend and physician of Augustus. This clan name, of unknown origin, could also be the source of Arthur.

In more recent times Arthur enjoyed a great spell of popularity in Britain towards the end of the nineteenth century. It survived longer in Scotland than elsewhere, being the 33rd most frequently given boys' name in 1935, 65th in 1958. Since then its use has continued to decline.

Black *(Surnames of Scotland)* quotes a letter written by Arthur Laurenson in 1879 about the use of Arthur in the Shetlands:

'The forename Arthur is common in Shetland now, but I rather think it is only a 17th or 18th century corrupt form of the Old Northern **Ottar.** Last century **Otto** or **Otho** or **Ottie** was a frequent forename here, and now no case of it occurs. In our North Isles it has even been Judaised into **Hosea,** so that Otto Ottoson was transmuted into Hosea Hoseason—so written, but pronounced 'Osie Osieson.'

In 1958 one Scottish girl was called **Arthurina.**

Athol(l) (m)   Atholl, 'New Ireland,' is a district in Perthshire which gave rise to a Scottish surname. Atholl and Athol both occur occasionally as Christian names. The original meaning of the placename is obscure.

Audrey (f)   A shortened form of an Old English name composed of two elements, 'noble' and 'strength.' The name was occasionally used in the nineteenth century, then it became fashionable in the period 1920-30. In 1935 it was

still ranked 44th in Scotland, but it has faded away since
then.

Aulay (m)   A form of Gaelic **Amhlaibh,** which in turn
represents a Scandinavian name appearing variously as
Ola, Olaf, Olav, Olavi, Olof, Oluf, Ole and **Olle.**
The Old Norse form of the name was **A(n)leifr,** which
indicates that it was originally composed of elements
meaning 'ancestor' and 'relics.' In his book, *The Shetland
Isles,* A. T. Cluness tells us that the name Olaf was frowned
upon by the authorities as part of a policy to weaken
Shetland's ties with Norway. The islanders were encouraged
to use **Oliver** as an English substitute, though some
parents (especially the *Macaulays*) have insisted on reverting
to Aulay or to Olaf, Olav, etc. In Ireland the original
Norse name became **Amhlaoibh,** which was rendered in
English as **Auliffe, Olave** or **Humphrey.** Black *(Surnames
of Scotland)* remarks that the Dumbartonshire Macaulays
derive their name from an Old Irish personal name
Amalghaidh, rather than Olaf. **Macaulay** is itself occasionally used as a Scottish Christian name.

Austin (m)   The usual form in medieval times of
Augustine, a diminutive of the Latin *augustus,* 'venerable.'
The name was made famous by St Augustine of Hippo,
the fourth-century bishop, author of the much-read *Con-
fessions*. The first archbishop of Canterbury also bore the
name. The use of Austin in Scotland, however, was helped
in former times by the similarity in sound between Austin
and the Gaelic **Uisdean** or **Huisdean.** Gaelic speakers used
it as an English substitute. Austin has also been long
established as a Scottish surname and this, too, contributes
to its modern use as a Christian name.

Avril (f)   A recent import from France, where it is the
name of the month 'April'. Since 1950 it has been used far
more frequently in Scotland than elsewhere in Britain. The

form **Avrille** occasionally occurs; and **April** itself has
shown signs of becoming more popular in the late 1970's.
Averil, however, the name of an Early English saint, is
composed of elements meaning 'boar' and 'battle.' This
name is sometimes used in Scotland.

B

Barbara (f) From a Greek word meaning 'strange,
foreign.' It is well used in Scotland, but a name common
to all Christian countries. In Scotland it was 16th most
frequently given name in 1858, 23rd in 1935, 42nd in 1958.
The name was immensely popular in the U.S.A. and
Canada from 1925-50, and in England and Wales from
1935-55. Diminutive forms include **Bab, Babs, Babbie,
Barbie** and, in Scotland, **Baubie.** See also **Annabella.**

Barry (m) Also **Barrie** (a form occasionally used for
girls). There is an Irish name **Bearach** or **Bearaigh,**
from *bear*, 'spear or javelin,' but use of this name in
Scotland is often a transference of the Scottish surname,
which in turn derives from the placename Barry (in Angus).

Bean (m) Gaelic **Beathan,** 'life.' Use of this personal
name in earlier times led to surnames such as *Macbean*
and *Macvean.*

Beathag (f) The feminine form of **Beathan** or **Bean.**
A later phonetic spelling is **Bethoc** (e.g. Bethoc, daughter
of Donald Bane, king of Scotland from 1093-7). **Beak**
is a later form. There has been occasional confusion with
the Old Testament name **Bithiah** or **Bethia** (Hebrew,
'daughter of Jehovah'). **Beatrice** was sometimes used as a
substitute for the name in Latin documents, and it has also

been 'translated' as **Sophia** (Greek, 'wisdom'). In fact, **Zoe** (Greek, 'life') would have been a more accurate translation.

Beatrice (f)   Latin, 'bringer of happiness.' As **Beatrix** this name was common in Scotland until the nineteenth century, and was still ranked 95th in 1935. It was occasionally written as **Bettrice,** and had the pet forms **Bea, Bee, Beatty, Trix** and **Trixie.**

Benjamin (m)   Hebrew, 'son of the right hand.' A nineteenth-century favourite in Scotland, and a name which has been very fashionable in the rest of the English-speaking world in the 1970's. In Scotland it was 75th most frequently used name in 1935, but by 1958 it was little used and subsequently it seems to have gone out of fashion completely. It is highly likely to return to favour in the 1980's.

Bernadette (f)   The feminine form of **Bernard.** This name is strongly associated with the Roman Catholic Church. It has been especially popular this century in Ireland and Scotland. It ranked 60th in Scotland in 1958.

Bernard (m)   A Germanic name composed of elements meaning 'a bear' and 'hard'. It is now unfashionable, but it was 51st most frequently used name in Scotland in 1935, 71st in 1958.

Blair (m)   A Scottish placename which became a surname, and is now occasionally used as a Christian name. Its original meaning according to Mackenzie *(Scottish Place Names)* was 'a plain, a clearing in a wood.'

Bonnie (f)   A popular girls' name recently in North America, where it is always explained as 'a Scottish name.' The word, of course, is Scottish, but the name has had little or no use in Scotland.

The following quotation from Margaret Mitchell's *Gone With the Wind* (1936) probably accounts for much of the name's use in modern times:

The name agreed upon for the child was **Eugenie Victoria,** but that afternoon Melanie unwittingly bestowed a name that clung . . . . Rhett leaning over the child had said: 'Her eyes are going to be pea green.'

'Indeed they are not,' cried Melanie indignantly . . . 'they are going to be blue . . . as blue as the bonnie blue flag.'

'Bonnie Blue Butler,' laughed Rhett, and Bonnie she became until even her parents did not recall she had been named for two queens.

Boyd (m)   Robert, grandson of Alan Fitz Flaald, was nicknamed *Buidhe,* 'yellow' because of the colour of his hair. He was the founder of the Scottish *Boyds*, though some Boyds owe their name to an ancestor who came from Bute. The surname is occasionally used as a Christian name in Scotland.

Bran (m)   Gaelic *bran,* 'raven.' Formerly in use in Scotland as a personal name.

Brenda (f)   A popular name in Scotland in the 1950's (it ranked 63rd in 1958). It was in vogue in England and North America rather earlier. Helena Swan mentioned Brenda in her *Girls' Christian Names* (1900), relating it to the Old Norse personal name **Brand,** 'sword.' She complained that 'the modern craving for unhackneyed names' had led it to gain ground steadily with the English public. She also suggested that Sir Walter Scott was responsible for introducing to a wider public what had previously been an exclusively Scottish name. Brenda is one of the heroines in his novel *The Pirate* (1821).

Brian (m)   A name long associated with Ireland because of the celebrated King Brian Boroimhe (926-1014), but it has been much used since 1925 in every English-speaking country. It ranked 47th in Scotland in 1935, 9th in 1958, going out of fashion in the late 1970's. It is usually spelt *Brian,* but **Bryan** occurs. The original meaning of the name is obscure.

Bridget (f)   Originally an Irish name, **Brighde, Bride,** meaning 'high one.' It was much used in Scotland in the 1930's but is now out of fashion. It was occasionally given in its Irish form **Brigid.** The diminutives **Bridie** and **Breda** were also used as independent names. Another pet form is **Biddy,** which in dialect became the word for a fowl.

Broderick (m)   Broderick is only occasionally used in Scotland as a Christian name, but it has come to be thought of as typically Scottish. It is tempting to associate it with **Roderick,** as do Johnson and Sleigh *(The Harrap Book of Boys' and Girls' Names).* They think it means 'son of Roderick' via the Welsh '*ap* Roderick' (*ap* was a later form of *map,* cognate with *mac* in Gaelic, 'son of'). However, the truth probably lies elsewhere. *Broder* and *Broderick* are Irish surnames which were brought to Scotland. Black *(Surnames of Scotland)* does not mention them, but MacLysaght *(The Surnames of Ireland)* remarks that both are derived 'from a Norse forename.' He presumably has in mind Norse **Brodhir,** modern Swedish **Broder** or **Bror,** 'brother.' This was at first a role name given to second or subsequent sons until it became a name in its own right.

Broderick was much publicised by the American actor, Broderick Crawford, who appeared in many films from 1937 onwards, and won an Oscar in 1949. The surname-origin was clearly demonstrated in his case, his mother's maiden name being Helen Broderick.

Bruce (m)   This famous surname, which derives from a Norman placename, has been much used as a Christian name in Scotland since 1930. In 1958 it was still ranked 64th. The name has also had intensive usage in the U.S.A. and Canada, but the English and Welsh have virtually ignored it as a name for their sons, making it instead a favourite choice for their dogs.

Bryce (m)   A common personal name in Scotland in the twelfth and thirteenth centuries, leading to its use as a surname (also as *Brice*). The name is found as early as the fifth century as **Bricius** (a Gaulish saint). Bryce is now occasionally used in Scotland as a Christian name.

C

Cairns (m)   A Scottish surname derived from a place-name, probably the lands of Cairns in the parish of Mid-Calder, Midlothian, as Black *(Surnames of Scotland)* suggests. A 'cairn' is a heap of stones which is raised over a grave, of which acts as a landmark. Cairns is occasionally used in Scotland as a Christian name.

Callum, Calum (m)   These are forms of St Columba's name in Gaelic, Calum being more usual. Both are used quietly but consistently in Scotland as Christian names, and as pet forms of **Malcolm.**

Cameron (m)   This Scottish surname, now frequently used as a Christian name in Scotland and elsewhere in the English-speaking world, is usually explained as Gaelic *cam shron,* 'crooked nose.' Black *(Surnames of Scotland)* thinks this may be true of the Highland clan name, but suggests that as a Lowland surname it may derive from a placename meaning 'crooked stream.'

Campbell (m)   Gaelic **Caimbeul,** 'crooked mouth.' A clan name which has been used since the 1930's in Scotland as a Christian name.

Cara (f)   In some cases this is the same name as **Kara,** but see separate entry under that name. Cara is a name that has appeared fairly recently in English-speaking countries, including Scotland. It is fast becoming popular. It possibly derives from the Italian endearment *cara,* equivalent to 'dear one.' Another possible source is Gaelic *caraid,* 'friend,' though this word normally implies a male friend. Browder *(The New Age Baby Name Book)* lists the name as Vietnamese for 'diamond' or 'precious gem,' but this should be dismissed as an exotic linguistic coincidence.

Carol, Carole (f)   These are shortened forms of **Caroline** which were popularised in the U.S.A. in the 1920's and later became highly fashionable throughout Britain. Carol was 11th most frequently used name in Scotland in the 1958 count, when 892 girls received the name. A further 175 Scottish girls were named Carole that year. (Others were called **Caroll, Carrol** and **Caryl.**) Carol has been well used in Scotland in the late 1970's, but it is clearly going out of fashion.

Caroline (f)   The feminine form of **Charles** (Latin **Carolus**). The name was popular in the nineteenth century in Scotland, then faded away somewhat in the early part of this century. It has been well used again in the 1970's. **Carolyn** is a modern spelling of the name which was briefly fashionable in the 1960's. Other forms used occasionally include **Carolyne, Carolynn, Carolynne.** The Latinised **Carolina** is rarely used in Scotland.

Carroll, Carroll (m)   A Scottish surname occasionally used as a male Christian name. It is said to have referred

originally to the Irish personal name **Cearbhall,** *not* to
Charles, as one might imagine.

Cathal (m) An ancient Celtic name meaning 'battle
mighty,' the use of which in earlier times led to surnames
such as *Macall, Maccall, Mackall* (Gaelic *MacCathail*).

Catherine (f) This name began as a word of unknown
origin but was early associated with a Greek word meaning
'pure.' In Greek the name begins with a *k;* in languages
such as French and Italian it begins with *c.* Since its introduction into the English-speaking world both spellings have
been used, together with internal variations as seen in
Catharine. Some of the forms used in Scotland in 1958,
with the number of their occurrences indicated, were:
Catherine, 1256; **Kathryn,** 77; **Katherine,** 72;
Katharine, 12; **Kathrine,** 7; Catharine, 2; **Kathrynn,** 1.
In a 1975 count the spelling *Katharine* appeared to be
gaining ground.
   The spelling confusion extends to **Kathleen** (Irish
Caitlin), a diminutive of Catherine. This can appear also
as **Kathaleen, Kathalien, Katheleen, Kathieleen,
Kathlen, Kathlyn, Cathaleen, Cathelene, Catheline,
Cathleen.**
   Catherine is a favourite name throughout the Christian
world. In Scotland it was in 9th position in 1858, and still
6th in 1958. Only a handful of names manage to survive
such intensive and consistent usage. Kathleen, although still
associated with Ireland, has also been much used in Scotland
since the 1930's. It was immensely popular in England
around 1925, and may have come from there as well as
Ireland. Different pet forms of Catherine and Kathleen
have been popular at different times, and have often been
used as independent names. **Kay (Kaye)** was fairly popular
in the 1950's, for example, and in the 1970's **Kerry
(Kerrie)** has fast gained ground. **Kit** and **Kitty** have

now largely been replaced by **Kate, Katie (Katy, Katey), Cathie (Cathy, Kathy).**

See also **Catriona** and **Karen.**

Catriona (f) The Gaelic form of **Catherine** or **Katharine.** It occurs also as **Caitriona,** which is the Irish spelling, and in the phonetic forms **Catrina** or **Katrina. Katrine, Katarina, Katriona** and **Katrena** are also found, as well as the Italian **Caterina.** In spite of this variety the name seems to be settling down as either Catriona or Katrina, both of which have been fairly popular with Scottish parents in the late 1970's. Robert Louis Stevenson's novel *Catriona* (1893) has undoubtedly had considerable influence both on usage and spelling.

Cecilia (f) A feminine form of **Cecil,** which itself derives from a Latin word meaning 'blind'. An alternative spelling is **Cecelia,** of which **Celia** is a diminutive. Other names from the same source are **Cicely, Cecily, Cecile** and **Cissie.** The Irish version of the name is **Sile,** anglicised as **Sheila, Sheela,** etc. Cecilia was most used in Scotland in the nineteenth century, but its use has declined slowly since then. Roman Catholic parents have remained most faithful to it, no doubt because of St Cecilia, the patron saint of music and of thè blind.

Cedric (m) The name of a character in Sir Walter Scott's *Ivanhoe* (1820) and later that of the hero in Frances Hodgson Burnett's *Little Lord Fauntleroy* (1886). E. G. Withycombe *(Oxford Dictionary of English Christian Names)* has suggested that Scott made a mistake and meant to use the name **Cerdic,** which is identified with Welsh **Ceredig,** 'amiable.' Trefor Davies *(A Book of Welsh Names)* suggests instead that the Celtic name **Cedrych** was simplified by Scott. Specialist students will find a long and highly technical discussion of the name in Ekwall's *English River Names*. The name Cedric was still being given to boys born in Scotland in 1958, but it has never been especially fashionable.

Charles (m)   The Germanic equivalent of **Andrew,** meaning 'a man,' or 'manly.' Charles was very popular in Scotland, as elsewhere in the English-speaking world, until 1950, but it has now fallen out of favour. It was a royal name of the House of Stewart, and much romanticised by the Jacobites. The feminine forms **Charlean, Charleen, Charlene** and **Charline** have all been used in Scotland (suggesting another possible source of **Arlene**). In Gaelic Charles in rendered as **Tearlach,** which resembles it in sound but means 'well-shaped.'

Charlotte(f)   A feminine form of **Charles,** introduced to Britain from Europe in the seventeenth century. It was popular in Scotland in the nineteenth century but has been steadily falling out of favour since the 1920's. An outstanding writer on names (as well as a highly successful novelist) was Charlotte Yonge, who published her *History of Christian Names* in 1863. She is modest about her own name, mentioning such diminutives as **Lotty** and **Chatty.** In France **Lolotte** was used. George Eliot has a **Totty** in *Adam Bede* (1859), a further corruption of Lotty, but this is described as 'more like a name for a dog than a Christian child.' Charles Dickens has a character Charlotte Tuggs who, when her family comes into money, immediately announces that henceforth she will be known as **Charlotta,** so it is possible that the Latinised form had upper-class associations at that time.

Chrisselle (f)   A blend of **Christina Isabella** used in Lewis. A correspondent, Mrs Joan Stewart, who reports on name usage in the Western Isles, also comments that many double Christian names in use there are pronounced in full, as **Mary Ann,** etc., or are slightly blended, so that **John Norman** and **John Neil** become *J' Norman, J' Neil.*

Christina, Christine (f)   Gaelic **Cairistiona.** Feminine forms of **Christian,** a name which has recently begun to be fashionable again in English-speaking countries. (Christian has been used for boys *and* girls in Scotland, elsewhere it is usually male.) Christina was the usual Scottish form of the name in the past, but this has now been overtaken by Christine. In 1958 usage in Scotland was as follows: Christine, 791; Christina, 319; Christian (f), 7; Christian (m), 4. **Christean, Christeen** and **Christene** were also used once each. The form of the name popularised by John Bunyan in his *Pilgrim's Progress* (1678) was **Christiana,** and this is also used occasionally in Scotland. Yet another form favoured by Scottish parents is the Scandinavian **Kirsten,** found also as **Kirsteen, Kirstan, Kirstine, Kristin** and **Kristine.** The pet forms **Chris, Chrissie, Christy, Kirsty, Kirstie, Kris** and **Kristy** are occasionally given as independent names. In the Orkneys **Teenie** is a diminutive form. **Tina** is more generally used in Scotland. Of these forms, *Christy (Christie)* may reflect the use of the Scottish surnames, which relate to ancestors who were named Christian or **Cristinus.**

In R. L. Stevenson's *Weir of Hermiston* occurs the passage:

'Miss Kirstie,' he began.

'Miss Christina, if you please, Mr Weir,' she interrupted. 'I canna bear the contraction.'

'You forget it has a friendly sound for me.'

Both Christina and Christine were predominantly Scottish and Irish names in the nineteenth century and the first part of the present century. By 1950, however, Christine had swept through the U.S.A. and Canada. It was also the 3rd most frequently used girls' name in England and

Wales. Since that time both forms of the name have been going out of fashion in Scotland and elsewhere, while Christian as a boys' name gains ground.

Christopher (m)   Gaelic **Gille Criosd.** One of the most popular names of the 1970's in every English-speaking country, though Scottish parents have perhaps been less enthusiastic about the name than their counterparts elsewhere. Nevertheless, it was already 40th most frequently used name in Scotland in 1958, and it has become more popular since. The name means 'one who carries Christ,' i.e., in his heart, but it was interpreted literally in earlier times and led to the story of St Christopher carrying the Christ child across the river.

A Scottish version of Christopher in former times was **Chrystal** or **Cristal**—as Cristal Nixon in Scott's *Red-gauntlet* (1824)—which gave rise to surnames such as *Christal, Crystal, Maccristal*. The diminutive was **Christie** or **Christy,** often pronounced *Crystie*. **Kit** was another diminutive: St Kitts in the West Indies was so named because Columbus wished to honour his patron saint.

Claire (f)   The immense popularity of this name in England in the 1970's has influenced Scottish parents, who are now using the name as never before. Claire is the French form of Latin **Clara,** though the latter appears more often in English as **Clare.** The name derives from a word meaning 'clear' or 'bright'. Derivatives include **Clarissa**—made famous in the eighteenth century by Samuel Richardson's novel, *Clarissa Harlowe* (1744)— **Clarice** and **Claribel.** Robert Burns wrote a poem to **Clarinda,** 'mistress of my soul.' In the nineteenth century Clara was a popular form. This had the Gaelic form **Sorcha,** 'bright.'

Clark (m)   This Christian name derives from the surname, which in turn indicates an ancestor who was a clerk—

a word which, when surnames were first used, meant a
'clergyman' or 'scholar.' The surname has been established
in Scotland since the twelfth century. There is little doubt,
however, that the immensely popular American actor Clark
Gable (1901-60: born William Clark Gable) had some
influence on the use of the name. In the 1940's and
50's it was being used in the U.S.A. and Canada, as well as
Scotland, but English parents have never taken to it.

Clementina (f)   Also **Clementine.** Feminine forms of
Clement, which derives from Latin *clemens*, 'mild,
merciful.' All three forms of the name are now rarely
used in Scotland, though the regular occurrence of
Clementina in the clan histories shows it to have been
formerly popular.

Clyde (m)   From the name of the River Clyde, and
used as a Christian name mainly by black Americans. It
almost certainly came to them from Scotland, thanks to
the habit amongst plantation owners (as well as slave traders)
of giving slaves geographical names as personal names. For
a brief history of such slave-naming and its subsequent
developments see the relevant chapter in my *First Names
First* (1977).

Colin (m)   In Scotland this name represents Gaelic
Cailean, which Black *(Surnames of Scotland)* describes as
'a personal name more or less peculiar to the *Campbells,*
the chief being always in Gaelic *MacCailein.*' Woulfe
(Irish Names for Children) suggests that the origin of this
Gaelic name is a word meaning 'whelp,' i.e., 'a youth.'
   In England the name derives ultimately from **Nicholas.**
Colin was used in England and Wales in the 1950's but
has since faded away. Scottish parents remain totally
faithful to it. The name was ranked 19th in Scotland in
1858, 17th in 1958. A count made in 1975 shows that it is now
one of Scotland's top ten names.

Cornelius (m) A name more associated with Ireland, where it anglicises **Conchobhar,** 'high will.' It also occurs as **Connor.** Cornelius was 91st most frequently used name in Scotland in 1935. It is now rarely used. It derives from a Roman clan name of obscure origins.

Cosmo (m) Introduced to Scotland in the seventeenth century by the 2nd Duke of Gordon, whose friend was **Cosimo III,** Grand Duke of Tuscany. The name is connected with 'cosmos' and 'cosmic;' its original Greek meaning being 'an ordered system.' Cosmo is only used occasionally in modern times.

Craig (m) This surname turned Christian name was once distinctively Scottish in the latter role, but it has swept through England and Wales in the late 1970's. The surname derived from 'craig,' the Scots form of 'crag' or 'cliff' (Gaelic *creag*). Scottish parents have been using the Christian name in ever-increasing numbers since 1945.

Crawford (m) A Lanarkshire placename which became a surname, now used in Scotland as a first name. The original meaning of the name may have been 'a ford where crows gather.'

Crighton (m) This is another Scottish surname occasionally used as a Christian name. It derives from the old barony of Crighton in Midlothian. Johnston *(Place Names of Scotland)* suggests an original meaning of 'border village.'

Cuthbert (m) This name was formerly very popular in the Lothians, where St Cuthbert (*c.* 634-87) was much admired—he was bishop of Lindisfarne from 685-7. The saint's name was Old English, composed of elements meaning 'famous, known' and 'bright.' Kirkcudbright was named for him, and reveals the common pronunciation of

the name, *Cudbert*. This led to diminutives such as
Cuddie, Cuddy. There is a Cuddy Headrigg, for instance,
in Scott's *Old Mortality* (1816). In general speech, however,
'cuddy' became the word for a stupid person and the nickname for a donkey. At one time Cuthbert was also the
name given to someone who tried to evade military
service. In the circumstances it is hardly surprising that
the name fell out of use.

Cyril (m) A name much in vogue from 1900-25. It
derives from a Greek word meaning 'lord.' It was ranked
94th in Scotland in 1935, but is now very rarely used.

D

Daniel (m) Hebrew, 'God has judged,' or 'God is my
judge.' The name was far more popular in Scotland and
Ireland during the nineteenth century than in any other
English-speaking countries. By 1925, however, it had also
become one of the top names in the U.S.A. It has since
spread to England and Wales, where it is among the most
frequently used names of the 1970's. In Scotland, Daniel
was in 22nd place in 1858, a position it retained until 1935.
By 1958 it had slipped to 41st place, and it appears for the
moment to be completely out of fashion. The present
intensive usage in England and Wales may bring about its
restoration. One possible reason for Daniel's early use in
Scotland is that it was erroneously thought to translate
Domhnall, or **Donald.**
    Feminine forms such as **Danielina** and (more frequently)
Danielle are used by Scottish parents.

Darren (m) A name of obscure origin, a surname before
it became in the early 1960's a much-used Christian name.
This appears to have been partly due to the use of the

name for a character in a television series called *Bewitched*.
Frank Thompson, a correspondent in New York, has suggested that the popular singer Bobby Darren may also
have had an influence on the use of the name.

David (m) Hebrew, 'beloved.' One of the all-time
favourite names in Scotland since the time of David I
(1084-1153). The Americans have also used it with great
intensity and consistency for at least a century. In England
and (of course) Wales where the name has been in use for
nearly a thousand years, it was used more and more after
1925 until it became top name in 1944. It stayed at or very
near the top of the popularity charts until 1961, and is
still much used.

Meanwhile, in Scotland, the name rose from 7th position
in 1858 to 4th place in 1958, when it was the name given
to one boy of every eighteen born in Scotland. It has
continued its remarkable run into the 1970's, as a count
made in 1975 clearly indicates.

If the Scots cannot claim David for themselves, they
have almost a complete monopoly of the feminine forms,
Davina, Davidina and **Davida.** Diminutives of these,
Vida and **Vina,** are also given occasionally as independent
names. Apart from the obvious surnames which derive
from David, names like *Daw, Dawe, Dawes* and *Dawson*
also owe their origin to obsolete diminutive forms. The
Gaelic form of David, **Dabhaidh,** led to surnames such as
Day and *Dey*.

Dawn (f) Scottish parents showed sudden interest in this
name in the 1950's, but they have now left it aside. In
England and Wales it is very much a name of the 1970's.

Deborah (f) Hebrew, 'a bee.' The name is now frequently
spelt **Debra.** It became a sudden favourite throughout the
English-speaking world in the 1950's, helped along by the
publicity given to it by such actresses as Deborah Kerr

and Debbie Reynolds. It is now disappearing, in Scotland
as elsewhere, almost as quickly as it arrived. **Debbie**
sometimes occurs as an independent name, and **Debora**
is also found.

Deirdre (f) The name of a legendary Irish heroine,
whose beauty was compared to that of Helen of Troy. The
origin of the name is obscure. William Sharp (*alias* Fiona
Macleod) introduced the name to Scottish readers in 1903,
when he published his novel *Deirdre*. It has been quietly but
consistently used in Scotland since then. In 1958, 36 girls
born in Scotland received the name; others were called
Deirdrie and **Dierdre.**

Denholm (m) A placename in Roxburghshire which be-
came a Scottish surname. It is occasionally used as a
Scottish Christian name. An alternative form is **Denham.**
The original meaning was probably 'settlement in a valley.'

Denis, Dennis (m) **Dionysus,** or 'lame god,' was the
ancient god of wine, also known to the Greeks and Romans
as *Bacchus.* The first bishop of Paris, later to become the
patron saint of France, was Dionysius (in Latin), Denis or
Denys (in French). The name was introduced to Britain
from France by the Normans.

In Scotland the name was most used in recent times in the
1920's and 30's. It was still well enough used in 1958 to be
included in the top hundred boys' names, the spelling
Denis at that time being slightly preferred to *Dennis.*

Sir Walter Scott refers to Dennis (his spelling) in *Guy
Mannering* (1815) as a 'Christian and crusading' name.

Denise (f) The French feminine form of **Denis.** It
enjoyed a spell of popularity in Scotland in the 1950's but
now seems to be little used.

Derek (m)   First found in English as **Dederick,** which shows its relationship to the Dutch **Diederick,** German **Dietrich** (earlier **Theodorich**). This consists of elements meaning 'people' and 'ruler.' Derek, also spelt **Derrick,** became very popular in England and Wales in the 1920's. By 1935 it was also being well used in Scotland, eventually becoming 20th most frequently used name in 1958. Derek continues to be a favourite name in Scotland, though it is no longer fashionable in England and Wales. Scottish parents sometimes use the spellings **Dereck, Derick, Deryk** and **Derik** as well as Derrick. Scott has a character in *Guy Mannering* (1815) who bears another Dutch form of the name, **Dirk.**

Desmond (m)   A mainly Irish name which was also being used in England and Wales in the 1920's. In Scotland it was used to some extent between 1930 and 1960. Desmond is an Irish placename and surname as well as a Christian name.

Diana, Diane (f)   Diana was identified by the Romans with the Greek *Artemis,* goddess of light and the moon. The French form of her name, Diane, suddenly became popular in all English-speaking countries around 1950. In Scotland, for instance, it appeared from nowhere to become 48th most frequently used name in 1958. **Dianne** was also used, but many Scottish parents preferred the original Latin form, Diana, which Scott also favoured for the heroine of *Rob Roy* (1817). **Dianna** is a rare variant, as is **Deanna.** The latter form was made known by the Canadian actress and singer Deanna Durbin. Diane Cilento and Diana Dors are other actresses who may have helped bring their names into wider use.

As with so many names, the sudden spell of popularity has been followed by an almost equally sudden rejection. Diane and Diana are now hardly used.

Diarmid(m)   Clan *Campbell* was originally known as Clan *Duibhne*, deriving from Diarmid O' Duin. He took his name from the mythological Diarmid, the Achilles of Celtic legend, who is said to be buried in Glen Lonain, Argyllshire, among other places. Black (*Surnames of Scotland*) explains the name as 'unenvious.' In Ireland, where the name is far more commonly used, the name occurs as **Diarmaid, Dermid, Dermod** or **Dermot. Jeremiah** and **Jeremy** are used as English substitutes. The name gave rise to many Scottish surnames, including *MacDairmid, MacDearmid, MacDermaid, MacDermont.*

Donald(m)   In some ways Donald is the most Scottish of names, yet this century it has undoubtedly been far more intensively used in the U.S.A. and Canada than in Scotland itself. The Scots, of course, established the name as their property in the preceding centuries, and it will always be associated with the Clan *Donald.* In modern Gaelic the name is **Domhnall**, and there is general agreement as to its original meaning of 'world mighty.'

   Donald was the 16th most frequently used name in Scotland in 1858, 19th in 1935, 25th in 1958. The most recent count (1975) shows that its use as a Christian name continues to decline. Feminine forms derived from it include **Dona, Donalda** and **Donaldina.** The use of **Donna** for girls may also be influenced by a supposed relationship to the name. See also **Daniel.**

Donna (f)   Italian, 'lady, mistress.' A fashionable name in the 1970's throughout Britain. In Scotland other Italian names, such as **Donata** and **Donatella,** are occasionally used. One also finds **Donetta, Donella, Donelle.** In many cases the wish to link with the (paternal) name **Donald** is likely to have influenced the choice.

Doreen(f)   This Irish name, which Woulfe (*Irish Names For Children*) explains as 'sullen,' was an immense success

in England and Wales in the 1920's. By 1935 it was also
38th most frequently used name in Scotland, though it
had dropped to 86th place by 1958. It is now very rarely
used. E. G. Withycombe, in her *Oxford Dictionary of
English Christian Names,* decides that it is a 'working-class'
name. Less arguably, she suggests that Edna Lyall's novel
Doreen (1894) was probably responsible for introducing the
name to a wider public.

Dorothy (f)   This Greek name, 'gift of god,' was suddenly
revived at the end of the nineteenth century in all English-
speaking countries. It then became one of the commonest
girls' names for some thirty years, but it has been completely
out of fashion since 1960. The Latinised **Dorothea** and
the diminutive **Dora** were often used. **Doll, Dolly, Dothy,
Dot, Dotty,** etc., are amongst the pet forms of the name,
which is rendered in Gaelic as **Diorbhàil.**

Douglas (m)   A Celtic river name, meaning 'dark blue,'
which became a Scottish surname, then a Christian name.
As such it has been well used this century, especially
during the period 1930-65. It is still in use, but can no
longer be considered fashionable. The name was exported to
England and Wales in the 1930's and later became popular
in North America.

No distinct feminine forms of the name seem to be used,
and Douglas in any case appears to have been a girls' name
in earlier times. Camden, writing in 1605, includes it in his
list of girls' names and compares it with **Jordan,** another
river name which was borrowed for use as a (male)
Christian name. The spelling **Douglass** (also a surname
form) is sometimes found, and **Douglasina** is occasionally
used for girls.

Drummond (m)   This well-known Scottish clan name
and surname derives from the barony of Drummond in
Stirlingshire. The name is a variant of the placename

Drymen, for which no satisfactory etymology can be offered. Drummond has been linked with Scottish history since the thirteenth century, and is fittingly used from time to time as a Christian name.

Dugald (m)   The usual Scottish form of Gaelic **Dughall,** though it also appears as **Dougal, Dougall** and **Dugal.** The name was originally used by the Irish to describe the 'black strangers,' i.e., the Danes. It is nowadays thought of as a characteristically Scottish name.

Duncan (m)   Gaelic **Donnchad,** 'brown warrior.' The name of two Scottish kings, one of whom was murdered by his cousin, *Macbeth.* Shakespeare's play on that subject has made the name Duncan widely known, but it has never been used very much in the U.S.A. The English and Welsh showed interest in the name in the 1960's, but they have since abandoned it. Duncan was the 15th most frequently used name in Scotland in 1858, but it had fallen to 51st place by 1958. An unofficial count made in 1975 indicated that it had by then fallen still lower in the ratings. It is also less common as a Scottish surname, ranking 33rd in 1958 but 44th in 1976.

E

Eachann (m)   A Gaelic name, 'horse lord,' usually 'translated' by the etymologically unrelated **Hector.** Its earlier form was **Eachd(h)onn.**

Edgar (m)   Old English *ead*, 'wealthy,' and *gar*, 'spear.' Eadgar, king of Scots, reigned from 1097-1107. The name later became a surname in Scotland and *Edgars* established themselves as extensive land-owners. The surname often took the form *Edzear*. Sir Walter Scott made Edgar,

Master of Ravenswood, the hero of his novel *The Bride of Lammermoor* (1819). He would have been especially familiar with the name because of its common occurrence in Dumfries and Galloway.

The name was most used in Scotland, as elsewhere in the English-speaking world, towards the end of the nineteenth century. In 1958, however, only three boys born in Scotland received the name. See also **Adair.**

Edith (f)   An Old English name composed of elements meaning 'rich, happy' and 'war.' The name was very popular in England and Wales from 1875-1925. It then faded away completely and has not so far been revived. The Scottish frequency lists for 1935 show Edith in 42nd position. In 1958, though it was no longer amongst the top hundred girls' names, 75 girls born in Scotland received this name.

Edna (f)   A Biblical name of unknown origin which was fashionable in Scotland, as elsewhere in the English-speaking world, in the 1930's. It is now little used.

Edward (m)   An Old English name composed of two elements meaning 'rich, happy' and 'guardian.' Its historical associations are mainly English, but the name has long been popular in other countries. In Scotland Edward ranked 30th in 1858 and 30th again in 1958. In between those two dates it rose in the 1930's to 18th position. The name continues to be used by Scottish parents but it is not particularly fashionable.

The Gaelic form of the name is **Eideard** and there are many pet forms, such as **Ed, Eddie, Eddy, Ned, Neddie, Neddy, Ted, Teddie, Teddy.**

Edwin (m)   An Old English name composed of elements that mean 'rich' and 'friend.' It is now little used in

Scotland, though it was 72nd most frequently used name in 1935.

Edwina (f)   A feminine form of **Edwin** that has been more used in Scotland than any other English-speaking country. **Edweena** is sometimes found.

Eileen (f)   Originally the same name as **Aileen,** though the latter is now often pronounced *Ay-leen*. The two spellings are almost equally popular in Scotland. In 1958, 264 girls were named Eileen, while 237 became Aileen. (In 1935 Eileen was used twice as often as Aileen.) Both forms of the name have been imported from Ireland, where the spelling confusion also exists, **Eibhilin** or **Eibhlin** having the variant **Aibhilin.** In one sense, Aileen is the more Scottish form of the name, for although Eileen became very popular in England and Wales in the 1920's, Aileen was almost unknown there. Eileen also appears to be the more usual modern Irish form. Occasionally found are the variants **Ilean, Ileene** and **Ilene.** The origin of the name is not clear, though it is often connected with **Helen** or **Evelyn.** Woulfe *(Irish Names for Children)* has suggested a derivation from **Avelina,** 'hazel nut.'

Eilidh (f)   A Gaelic form of **Helen** which has been used in the late 1970's in Scotland.

Elaine (f)   The Greek name **Helen,** 'the bright one,' was formerly **Helaine** in French, though the *H-* was not pronounced. This gave rise to Elaine, first mentioned by Sir Thomas Mallory in his *History of Prince Arthur* (1470). Tennyson (1809-92) was later to call one of his Idylls *Elaine*. In Scotland Elaine suddenly began to be used with great intensity around 1950. The indications are that it replaced **Ellen,** which fell from grace with equal suddenness around that time. Scottish parents still continue to use Elaine with great regularity, whereas in England and

Wales, where the name was also fashionable from 1950-65, it is now tending to disappear. **Ellaine** and **Elayne** are occasionally used in Scotland as variant spellings.

Eleanor (f)   A form of **Helen** which early became a royal name in England. It was frequently used there in the nineteenth century, whereas in Scotland it is very much a name of the twentieth century. It was most used in the 1930's, but it was still in 65th position in 1958. Variations and diminutives include **Elinor, Elenor, Ellenor, Lenore, Leonora, Nora, Norah.**

Elizabeth(f)   Hebrew, '(my) God is perfection' (or 'satisfaction'). The Gaelic is **Ealasaid.** One Scottish woman in every twenty-four bears this name, though there are signs that it has been going out of fashion since 1965. The name has also steadily declined in England and Wales, where it was a great favourite until the end of the nineteenth century, but it is still one of the most frequently used names in the U.S.A. In Scotland it was in 3rd position in 1858 and 1935. By 1958 it was in 2nd place. A count in 1975 showed it to have fallen away considerably. Elisabeth Inglis, discussing the names most frequently mentioned in birth announcements in the *Scotsman* during 1977 (*Scotsman*, January 4th, 1978) also shows that the name is no longer in the Scottish top ten.

Elizabeth has a great many pet forms which are often used as independent names. In 1958, for example, girls born in Scotland received the names **Bessie, Beth, Betty, Eliza, Elsbeth, Elsie, Elspeth, Lillibet, Lisa** and **Lizbeth.** Other Scottish girls were given foreign forms of the name or their diminutives: Spanish **Isabel,** French **Elisabeth, Lisbeth, Elise,** German **Lisa, Lise.** In earlier times Isabel and **Isabella** were in fact totally interchangeable with Elizabeth. The various pet forms have been popular at different times in Scotland. In the nineteenth century **Eliza** and **Betsy** were especially fashionable, and

were used rather more than the Scottish Elspeth (or
Elspet). By 1935 Elsie had come upon the scene, Elspeth
was being less used, and Eliza and Betsy were no longer
among the top hundred names. In the 1970's Lisa has been
the up-and-coming form, with **Bettina** also enjoying
a spell of popularity.

James Boswell makes a well-known comment about the
use of pet forms of Elizabeth in his *Life of Dr Samuel
Johnson* (1791). Mrs Johnson was an Elizabeth 'whom he
used to name by the familiar appellation of **Tety,** or **Tetsy,**
which, like Betty or Betsy, is provincially used as a contraction for Elizabeth.' This usage, continues Boswell,
seems ludicrous 'when applied to a woman of her age and
appearance.' This seems a little harsh. One might interpret
the use of such endearments by a speaker who was
notoriously formal in his speech as a gesture of great
tenderness.

Ellen (f) An English form of **Helen,** much used in
Scotland until the early 1950's, when **Elaine** became the
more fashionable form. Ellen was 32nd most frequently
used name in Scotland in 1858, 29th in 1935, but 79th in
1958. A count made in 1975 shows no trace of it.

Elliot (m) A Border surname occasionally used in Scotland as a Christian name. Black *(Surnames of Scotland)*
seems to confuse it with an Old English personal name
Aethelweard, which became the surname *Aylward.* Elliot
(also in the forms **Eliot, Eliott, Elliott**) is more likely
to be a diminutive of **Eli,** itself a shortening of **Elijah** or
Elias. Elias developed into **Ellis,** which also occurs occasionally as a Christian name in Scotland for girls as well
as boys.

Elma (f) In Scotland this is probably a diminutive of
Wilhelmina. E. G. Withycombe *(Oxford Dictionary of
Early Christian Names)* cites a special instance in the Earl of

Elgin's family where it was a blend of the mother's names, **Elizabeth Mary.** There is a male name **Elmo,** a pet form of **Erasmus,** but Elma is unlikely to be its feminine form.

Elsa (f) A German diminutive of **Elizabeth** (German **Elisabeth**) made known internationally by Wagner's *Lohengrin* (1850). Occasionally used in Scotland as an alternative to **Elsie.** See also **Ailsa.**

Elsie (f) This is usually assumed to be a short form of **Elizabeth.** In Scotland **Elshie** was a Lowland diminutive form of **Alexander,** but this form does not seem to have been used for **Alexandrina.** Elsie may also have been a shortening of **Elspeth,** or **Elspie** in Arthur Clough's poem, *The Bothy of Toberna-Vuolich* (1848).

The novel *Elsie Venner*, by Oliver Wendell Holmes, was published in 1861, and a few years later Longfellow made an Elsie the heroine of his *Golden Legend.* By 1875 Elsie was immensely popular in the U.S.A., and by 1900 it was being used in Britain in great numbers. In Scotland it was still ranked 64th in 1935, but by then it was going out of fashion.

Elspeth (f) A Scottish contraction of **Elizabeth,** often occurring as **Elspet. Elspie** is a pet form. Scott has characters of this name in *The Antiquary* (1816), *The Monastery* (1820) and *Guy Mannering* (1815). Elspet(h) was 36th most frequently used name in Scotland in 1858, 78th in 1935.

Emily (f) This is derived from the Roman clan name **Aemilius,** through its feminine form **Aemilia. Amelia** looks as if it should be the same name, and was often thought to be so in earlier times, but it derives from a Germanic name of uncertain origin. Aemilius was possibly an 'emulator,' or 'one who strives to equal or rival.' Emily was used to some extent in Scotland in the nineteenth century, but it has been out of fashion for some time. It is one of the 'old' names, however, which has been restored to use in many English-speaking countries in the late 1970's.

Emma (f)   This was originally a short form of such Germanic names as **Irmgard,** itself from **Irmingard.** The first element in such names meant 'all embracing.' In the nineteenth century Emma was very popular in England and Wales, less so in Scotland. It has returned in force fairly recently, its renewed popularity apparently coinciding with a television series called *The Avengers*, featuring a character called Emma Peel. Jane Austen's novel *Emma* (1816) is often used in English classes at school.

Ena (f)   In Scotland this is used from time to time as a variant of **Ina,** but the Irish Ena derives from a feminine form of **Aed.**

Eric (m)   A Norse and Germanic name, meaning 'ruler,' perhaps 'sole ruler.' Although introduced to a wide public by the novel *Eric: or Little by Little* (1858) by Dean Farrar, the name only really began to be well used in England and Wales in the 1920's. It enjoyed a brief spell in the limelight but soon faded. Scottish parents came to the name a little later, and it was still 36th most frequently used name in Scotland in 1935. By 1958 it was down to 60th place, and in the 1970's it has been totally out of fashion. The well-known philologist Eric Partridge (born 1894) says of it in *Name This Child*: 'As I discovered at school, Eric was despised as pretty-pretty.'

Erica (f)   Also **Erika.** Feminine forms of **Eric** or **Erik,** though *erica* also happens to be the Latin botanical name for 'heather.' They are quietly used in Scotland, sometimes to represent Gaelic **Oighrig** or **Eithrig** (see **Africa**).

Ernest (m)   The name has the meaning of the word

'earnest' in a phrase like 'to do something in earnest.'
Ernest was much used in England and Wales between 1875
and 1925, during which period it was also a favourite with
Scottish parents. By 1935 it was fast losing ground in
Scotland, though it was still ranked 57th. Oscar Wilde's
Importance of Being Earnest was first performed in 1895.
Erna and **Ernestina** occur occasionally as feminine forms.

Esmé (f)　Formerly a boys' name also. It was introduced
to Scotland from France in the sixteenth century by the
Duke of Lennox, Esmé Stewart d'Aubigny, cousin of
James VI, whose mother was French. The name appears
to be the past participle of Old French *esmer*, 'to esteem.'
It is a decidedly Scottish name as far as the English-
speaking world is concerned, having been more used by
Scottish parents in the past than those elsewhere; but even
in Scotland it is now little used.

Esther (f)　In former times this name could interchange
with **Hester,** but Esther is the main Scottish form. In the
Old Testament Esther is the Persian name of the Jewish
captive *Hadassah*, 'myrtle.' It is not clear whether the one
name translates the other. Esther has often been linked
with the Persian word for 'star.' Jonathan Swift certainly
did so when he wrote to Esther Johnson as **Stella,** which
is Latin for 'star.'

Esther was 80th most frequently used name in Scotland
in 1935. It had been fashionable somewhat earlier in
England and Wales, as well as in North America. Pet
forms of the name include **Essie** and **Hetty.** The latter is
used occasionally as an independent name.

Ethel (f)　A name that was most used in Scotland from
1875-1925. It had been made popular by novels such as
The Newcomes, by Thackeray, and *The Daisy Chain,* by
Charlotte Yonge, both published in the 1850's. It was a
shortened form of various names beginning with the element

Ethel-, such as **Ethelinda, Ethelred.** Ethel itself means 'noble.'

Euphemia (f) Greek, 'well spoken of.' The name of a saintly martyr, and a name which has been used far more often in Scotland—where it occurs frequently in the histories of the Scottish clans—than in any other English-speaking country. It was the 20th most frequently used name in Scotland in 1858, 39th in 1935. In 1958, however, only 35 Scottish girls were given the name, and none received its Gaelic form, **Oighrig.** In earlier times, when its diminutive **Effie** was commonly heard, it became confused with the Gaelic name which is anglicised as **Africa.**

The best-known literary Euphemia is **Effie** Deans, in Scott's *Heart of Midlothian* (1818). Robert Burns serenaded **Eppie** Adair, which shows another diminutive of the name—one also used by George Eliot in *Silas Marner* (1861), though in her case it was used as a pet form of **Hephzibah.** The **Phemie** in A. J. Cronin's *Hatter's Castle* (1931) is really a Euphemia. **Etta, Euphan, Euphie** and **Fanny** occur as other pet forms.

H. G. Wells made gentle fun of the name in *Kipps* (1905). When Kipps is about to become a father, and is discussing possible names with Buggins, he thinks of Euphemia, his mother's name.

'It isn't a name *common* people would give to a girl, is it?'

It isn't the name any decent people would give to a girl,' said Buggins, 'common or not.'

'Lor!' said Kipps. 'Why?'

'It's giving girls names like that,' said Buggins, 'that nine times out of ten makes 'em go wrong. It unsettles 'em.'

Gordon McGill, in his novel *Arthur,* recounts that as a small boy he thought his aunt had the single letter *F* as a Christian name. Later he discovers that she is being addressed as **Eph,** another short form of Euphemia.

Eva (f)   Also **Eve,** which is the English form of Latin *Eva*. Both derive from a Hebrew name traditionally explained as 'life' or 'lively.' But in earlier times Eva was used in Scotland as a substitute for the Gaelic **Eubha,** itself a form of an ancient Irish name, **Aoife,** of unknown origin. Canon Murdoch rightly says in his Introduction to *The Loyall Dissuasive* that formerly in Highland families there was always an Eva 'who had to account for things unaccountable.' The name constantly occurs in the clan histories. Eva is now no longer a common name in Scotland, but when it is used, Eva is still slightly preferred to Eve.

Evelyn (f)   This name became very popular in Scotland in the 1920's. It was still 28th most frequently used name for girls in 1935, but it had dropped to 66th position by 1958. It has occasionally been used as a male name, where it probably derives from the surname, itself a diminutive of Eve. A comment on the male use of Evelyn is to be found in Robert Heinlein's novel, *Glory Road*. It makes a general point as well as a particular one, and echoes to some extent the well-known comments of actor John Wayne, born Marion Morrison, about his real name:

My daddy had been proud of a couple of his ancestors— but is that any excuse for hanging 'Evelyn Cyril' on a male child? It had forced me to learn to fight before I could read.

The girls' name also occurs as **Evalyn, Evelina, Eveline, Evelynn, Evelynne, Evlyn, Evlynn,** though *Evelyn* is the usual spelling. The forms suggest that parents think of the name as **Eva** or **Eve,** both of which are also used in Scotland as independent names, plus an additional element. Ernest Weekley *(Jack and Jill)* saw the name as a derivative of Old French *aveline*, 'hazel nut.' E. G. Withycombe *(The Oxford Dictionary of English Christian Names)* links it with the German names **Avi** and **Avila.** Woulfe *(Irish Names for Children)* says that Evelyn

may derive, like **Eileen** and **Aileen,** from the name
Avelina. Whatever the origin, Evelyn is now little used by
Scottish parents.

Ewan (m) This is the preferred modern spelling in
Scotland of a name which also occurs as **Owen, Euan,
Ewen, Euen** and **Ewhen.** The Gaelic **Eoghann** is the
source of these forms. In early Latin documents Eoghann
was equated with **Eugenius** (**Eugene**), 'well-born,' and
this was traditionally regarded as the meaning of the name.
In some parts of Scotland **Hugh** was erroneously used as
a substitute for Eoghann. The real etymology of the Gaelic
name is obscure; all that can be said is that Eoghann
occurs in ancient Celtic history and legend and that it is
ultimately responsible for such surnames as *Macewan,
Macewen, Macewing,* etc. In former times *Ewen* was the
usual spelling of the Christian name. It was especially
associated with the *Camerons* and *Macphersons*. Eugene is
steadily used in modern Scotland.

F

Farquhar (m) Gaelic **Fearchar,** 'very dear one.' A Celtic
personal name which became a Scottish surname and gave
rise to the clan name *Farquharson*. It is occasionally used
as a Christian name.

Fenella (f) Sir Walter Scott used this form of the Gaelic
name **Fionnghal,** 'white shoulder,' in *Peveril of the Peak*
(1823), which has led some reference works to regard it as a
Scottish name. It has never been taken up in Scotland to
any great extent, however, perhaps because the character in
Scott's novel who bears it is severely handicapped. The
name occurs more frequently in Ireland, where it is usually
spelt **Finela** or **Finola** or abbreviated to **Nuala.** In former

times, when it was necessary for Gaelic speakers to use names familiar to English speakers, **Penelope** was often used as a substitute.

Fergus (m) Gaelic **Fearghas,** 'supreme choice.' A Celtic name which is now only in occasional use as a Christian name. It is also found in Scottish surnames such as *Ferguson* and *Macferries*. Some Fergusons claim descent from Fergus, Prince of Galloway, who ruled in the twelfth century.

Fife (m) This Scottish shire name is also a surname. Some families use it as a Christian name.

Finlay (m) Also **Findlay, Finley.** Gaelic **Fionnlagh,** 'fair hero.' The name of Macbeth's father. This ancient personal name became a Scottish surname which is also found as a Christian name. The *Farquharsons* are known in Gaelic as *Clann Fhionnlaigh*, 'descendants of Finlay,' the particular Finlay being Finlay Mór, deputy royal standard bearer at Pinkie in 1547.

Fiona (f) J. I. M. Stuart comments in his novel, *A Memorial Service*: 'although *Fiona* sounds eminently Scottish it is in fact scarcely a genuine name at all, having been invented in the nineteenth century by a man called William Sharp as part of a pseudonym.' The pseudonym referred to is Fiona Macleod, 'authoress' of many works of Celtic literature. Sharp eventually wrote 'her' biography for *Who's Who*. Several invented names have later become very popular throughout the English-speaking world (e.g. **Pamela, Lorna, Wendy, Vanessa**), and Fiona now joins their ranks. The name was in 10th position in Scotland in 1958, though it was not mentioned in the Scottish Registrar General's Report for 1935. It was also to be found in the 1950's in England, Australia and Canada. The name probably reached its peak in England around 1970, but it is

still being very much used in Scotland. It is based on the
Gaelic *fionn*, 'fair.' It has occasionally been used to
represent **Fionnghal** (see **Flora**).

Flora (f)   Latin, 'flowers.' The name of the Roman
flower goddess. Flora's early use in Scotland was probably
as a substitute for the Gaelic name **Fionnghal**, 'fair
shouldered,' (which led to Irish **Fenella, Finella**). Flora
Macdonald (1722-90) naturally comes to mind when the
name is mentioned, and she must have been responsible
for the name's rise to great popularity in Scotland. It
was still frequently used throughout the nineteenth century,
and even in 1935 it was the 51st most frequently used
name for girls. Its use has continued to decline since then,
and only 33 girls born in Scotland in 1958 received the
name. It probably survives now, like so many old
favourites, as a middle name. In literature there is Flora
MacIvor in Scott's *Waverley* (1814), while in his *Talisman*
(1825) he has a **Florise.**

The *Oxford Dictionary of English Christian Names* makes
the rather Johnsonian remark that Flora 'was formerly
considered (in England) a suitable name for a spaniel but not
for a woman.' This comment presumably derives from
Charlotte Yonge, who explains that a Spanish woman
called **Florinda,** but generally known as *la Cava*, 'the
wicked one,' was responsible for the dog-naming. Miss
Yonge also points out that Flora Macdonald often spelt her
own name as **Florie. Florrie** is still a diminutive form.

The televising of Galsworthy's *Forsyte Saga* in the 1960's
brought the name **Fleur** (French, 'flower') into use in
Scotland and elsewhere. **Flore** was in fact the earlier
French version of Flora.

Florence (f)   This is now used only as a feminine name
in Scotland, though formerly, as it still is in Ireland, it
was well known as a male name. Florence Wilson of Moray
was a famous Latin scholar in the sixteenth century, his

Christian name being rendered **Florentius** in Latin. In Britain its use mainly honoured Florence Nightingale (1820-1912). It was very popular in England from 1875-1925, but then died away. It followed roughly the same pattern in Scotland, arriving a little later but surviving longer. In 1935 it was the 65th most frequently used name in Scotland. The various diminutive forms, **Flo, Florrie, Flossie, Floy,** etc., do not seem to have been used as independent names.

Florence Nightingale received her name because she was born in the city of Florence, but the name had been used as a personal name in Roman times. It derives from the Latin *florens*, 'flourishing.'

Some remarks concerning the use of Florence and its pet forms occur in *Cards of Identity*, by Nigel Dennis:

'The hideous abbreviation "Florrie" may safely be used by you two, on account of your being creatures of tenderness, jollity and enthusiasm. To me, however, as master of the house, she must always be Florence . . . Florence is fraught with grave, inhibitory influence, Florrie is suggestive of loose hair and even misappropriation.'

Forbes (m)   Gaelic **Foirbeis.** An Aberdeenshire place-name meaning 'field, district,' which became a surname. Traditionally the *Forbes* clan descend from Ochonochar. He slew a bear which terrorised anyone who tried to live in Donside, the braes of Forbes. Once the bear had been disposed of Ochonochar and his family settled there. The name Forbes is occasionally used in Scotland as a Christian name.

Frances (f)   Gaelic **Frangag.** The feminine form of **Francis. Francesca** (the Italian equivalent), **Francina** and **Franca** are also used by Scottish parents. Frances was a Victorian name in England and Wales, with **Franny** and **Fanny** as its pet forms. In Scotland the name continued in use until recently (it was 45th most frequently

used name in 1958, having been in 43rd place in 1858). It
now seems to have gone out of fashion. **Frankie** rather
than Fanny is the modern diminutive, though the latter,
according to a character in Thackeray's *Pendennis* (1850),
was 'a very pretty little name.'

Francis (m)   From the Latin *Franciscus*, 'a Frenchman.'
This name was made generally known by St Francis of
Assisi (*c.* 1182-1226), whose real name was **John.** In
England and Wales Francis was most used in the nineteenth century. In Scotland it was ranked 25th in 1858,
16th in 1935, 34th in 1958. It has subsequently dropped
out of favour, but even so, Francis (and **Frank** used
as an independent name) has been used more intensively
in Scotland this century than in any other English-
speaking country.

Fraser (m)   **Frazer** also occurs, though *Fraser* is certainly
the more usual spelling in Scotland. The Gaelic form is
Friseal. This Scottish surname, now a popular Christian
name, not only in Scotland but in other English-speaking
countries, began as a French placename, which was variously
recorded as Frisselle, Freseliere, Fresel, etc. Bearers of the
surname saw it as deriving from French *fraise*, 'strawberry,'
which accounts for the flower of the strawberry plant
being used in the coat of arms. The original meaning of the
placename is unknown.

Freda, Frieda (f)   *Freda* is the more usual spelling in
Scotland, but *Frieda* is not unusual. It is usually a short
form of **Winifred,** but see also **Frederick.**

Frederick (m)   A name that was in 39th position in 1935,
and was still the 76th most frequently used name for boys
born in Scotland in 1958. In England and Wales it had
virtually disappeared after 1925, following a spell of great
popularity throughout the nineteenth century. The name is

of Germanic origin, composed of elements meaning 'peace' and 'ruler'. Feminine forms such as **Frederica** and **Frederickina** have been used in Scotland; **Freda** has no doubt also been used to link with the name.

Freya (f)   Freya was the ancient Norse goddess of love. Her name meant 'female ruler, mistress,' and it occurs also in the forms **Freyja, Freja** and **Froja.** The name of the god Odin's wife, **Frigga,** which gave rise to *Friday,* is *not* connected. Freya still occurs in Scotland, having formerly been a traditional name in Shetland.

G

Gail (f)   Also **Gael, Gale, Gayle.** This name is more American than British, but it was the 76th most frequently used name in Scotland in 1958, and it was clearly being well used in the late 1970's. It is a short form of **Abigail,** a Hebrew name meaning 'father rejoiced.' Abigail itself is showing signs of replacing Gail in England and Wales.

Garden (m)   A Scottish surname occasionally used as a Christian name. It derives from the barony of Gardyne in Angus, and is also found as **Gardin, Dalgarn,** etc.

Gary (m)   A modern name introduced to the English speaking world by Gary Cooper, the American actor, in the 1930's. It derives ultimately from the surname *Gary,* which is in turn from **Garret,** a form of **Gerard** still much used in Ireland. The use of Gary has increased in Scotland in the late 1970's, with **Garry** as a popular alternative— a spelling clearly influenced by the name of the Scottish river and glen.

Gavin (m) A name used by the *Dunbars*. Gavin Dunbar was archbishop of Glasgow and Lord Chancellor of Scotland in James V's reign. Another Gavin Dunbar was bishop of Aberdeen in the early sixteenth century. Gavin was a decidedly Scottish name until the 1960's, little used before that time in other English-speaking countries. It is now spreading rapidly in Australia and elsewhere. Black *(Surnames of Scotland)* says of it that it was 'a favourite forename throughout Strathclyde in past times. It is the Scots form of English **Gawayne,** in French **Gauvain.'** He also tells us that apart from being a common surname in Brechin in the seventeenth century it was to be found as such amongst 'the gypsies of the Border.' Its pet form is **Guy,** via **Gavie.**

Geoffrey (m) Also **Jeffrey.** Relatively little used in Scotland, though popular in England and Wales from 1925-50. Originally this was a Germanic name based on a word meaning 'peace.'

George (m) Greek, 'farmer, husbandman.' The 6th most frequently used name in Scotland in 1858, 6th in 1935, 10th in 1958. In spite of this long run of great popularity, the name has gone rapidly out of fashion since 1960. Scottish parents remained faithful to it longer than most. In England and Wales the name was intensively used during the nineteenth century, but it faded away after 1900. It has also been out of fashion in the 1970's in the other English-speaking countries. In Scotland its pet forms include **Geordie, Dod, Doddy,** and there are several feminine forms, the most popular being **Georgina.** The Gaelic forms are **Seòras, Seorsa** or **Deòrsa.**

Georgina (f) A feminine form of **George.** Other versions of the name used for Scottish girls include **Georgette, Georgia, Georgine** and **Georgena.** Earlier this century Georgina was a decidedly Scottish name in terms of usage.

It was ranked 31st in Scotland in 1935, having been placed 24th in 1858. By 1958, however, Georgina had dropped to 93rd position, and it subsequently almost disappeared. This situation is likely to change, as the name has become fashionable in England and Wales in the late 1970's. Georgia is the preferred form of the name in North America. (The name of the American state honoured King George II.)

Gerald (m) A Germanic name composed of elements meaning 'spear' and 'rule.' Gerald was the 55th most frequently used name in Scotland in 1935, and again in 1958. Since then it has tended to drop out of favour.

Geraldine (f) The feminine form of **Gerald.** In Scotland the name has never been especially popular, though it was used to some extent from 1925-60.

Gerard (m) A French version of the German name **Gerhard,** which was composed of elements meaning 'spear' and 'hard.' Gerard was in 84th position in 1935. By 1958 it was used slightly more often than **Gerald** in Scotland, which made it the 46th most frequently used name that year. The surname spelling **Gerrard** occurs occasionally as a Christian name. Gerard has been most used by the Scots and Irish, although there was a slight flurry of interest in it in England and Wales during the 1950's. An earlier colloquial form of the name was **Garret.** The feminine form **Gerardine** was used in Scotland in 1958.

Gilbert (m) A Germanic name, composed of elements meaning 'pledge' and 'bright.' Gilbert was 38th most frequently used name in Scotland in 1858, 63rd in 1935, but well out of the top hundred names by 1958. Black (*Surnames of Scotland*) says it was used as a substitute for **Gilbride** because of the accidental resemblance of the two names, though Gilbride means 'servant of St **Bridget.**'

The usual pet forms of Gilbert are **Gib, Gibb, Gibbie** and **Gil. Gibbon** was another form of the name, formerly popular in Perthshire. The Gaelic is **Gilleabart.**

Gilchrist (m)   Gaelic **Gille Criosd,** 'servant of Christ.' A common personal name in Scotland in the Middle Ages, still used by some Scottish families. It was formerly 'translated' as **Christopher.** In modern times *Gille Criosd* is reduced to **Crisdean.**

Giles (m, f)   The early popularity of St Giles, patron saint of cripples and beggars, is seen in the number of churches which are dedicated to him, including the High Kirk in Edinburgh. The name Giles comes through French **Gile** and **Gide** (surviving as surnames) from Latin **Egidius** or **Aegidius.** The Latin name derives in turn from a Greek word meaning 'kid.' The significance of this probably lies in the early use of kid leather for shields. In her *History of Christian Names,* Charlotte Yonge comments on the former use by 'Scottish ladies' of **Egidia.** This may have been the written form of a name that was still spoken as *Giles* until a spelling pronunciation replaced it. A notable example of such a Scottish lady, incidentally, was Miss Egidia Menzies, chieftainess of Clan *Menzies.* Giles was especially popular as a female name in the Edinburgh area in former times, no doubt because of the saint's role as patron of the city. One can compare the use of **Mungo** in Glasgow. In the Highlands Giles was thought of as an English equivalent of Gaelic **Sileas** or **Silis** (see **Julia**). Giles is now rarely used in Scotland and it has reverted to being a male name.

Gillanders (m)   Gaelic **Gillandreis,** 'servant of St Andrew.' Once a favourite personal name in Scotland, as were many names beginning with *gille.* This word originally meant 'youth,' later 'servant,' 'devotee.' It was prefixed to the names of popular saints (*Gilbride,* St

Bridget; *Gilzean,* St **John**; *Gillecalum,* St **Columba**; *Gillemartin,* St **Martin**; *Gilleonain,* St **Adamnan**). It is also found in *Gilchrist, Gillies* (for *gille Iosa,* 'servant of **Jesus**'), *Gilmore, Gilmour,* 'servant of the Virgin **Mary**.' In *Gillespie* we have 'the bishop's servant,' while in names like *Gilroy, gille* retains its original meaning of 'youth' and the complete name means 'red-haired boy.' Most of the names quoted will be familiar as Scottish surnames, and all are occasionally used as Christian names.

Gillean (m) Also **Gilian, Gilleon, Gillian, Gilzean, Gellion.** These forms also occur as Scottish surnames, pronounced with a hard *g* as in *give.* They derive from Gaelic *Gill' Eoin,* 'servant of St John.' Use of Gillian as a Christian name is said to be especially frequent in the Clan *Maclean.*

Gillian (f) This name is a form of **Juliana,** itself a feminine form of **Julius** (see **Julia**). Gillian was an immense success in England and Wales in the 1950's, though it has now faded away dramatically. In Scotland it seems to have arrived late, reaching only 59th position in the table of girls' names by 1958, but it has continued to be widely used in the 1970's. The diminutive **Jill** is often given as an independent name. The spellings **Jillian** and **Gilliane** also occur occasionally in Scotland.

Gladys (f) From the Welsh **Gwladys,** usually explained as a form of **Claudia.** In the 1870's Gladys was a rather exotic name, and one which was thought to be suitable for romantic heroines in novels such as *Gladys of Harlech,* by Anne Beale and *Gladys,* by Edith M. Dauglish. By 1900 it was one of the most frequently used names in Britain. It remained popular until the early 1930's, but it is now practically extinct. In Scotland it was in 63rd position in 1935, but it was obviously fading fast. It is now very rarely given.

Glen, Glenn (m)   Both forms of this name are used in Scotland, in almost equal numbers. It is a modern Christian name, and, in spite of its appearance, not particularly Scottish. There is evidence to suggest that it was first used in Canada, where it is still more popular than in other English-speaking countries. Scottish settlers in Canada may have used it first, in conscious allusion to Scottish glens, or it may have derived from the surname, which in turn derives from a placename. The actor Glenn Ford was born in Canada, though in his case Glenn replaced his real Christian name, **Gwyllyn. Glyn** is actually the Welsh equivalent of Glen.

Godfrey (m)   Germanic or Norse, 'god's peace.' An early Gaelic form of the name was **Gofraidh,** later **Goraidh,** commonly written as **Gorry.** According to Black *(Surnames of Scotland)* Goraidh 'is a common name in the West Highlands especially among the Macdonalds of Skye and the Macleods,' but this is probably no longer true.

Gordon (m)   Gaelic **Gòrdan.** A Berwickshire placename of uncertain origin gave rise to this surname and famous clan name, at one time that of the most powerful Scottish clan. As a Christian name it has been especially popular with Scottish parents this century. They made it their 25th most frequently used name in 1935 and 16th in 1958. The name has continued to be used a great deal in Scotland in the late 1970's. In England and Wales Gordon was most used between 1920 and 1940.

Grace (f)   Gaelic **Giorsal.** A decidedly Scottish name in terms of modern usage. In the 1950's, for example, the name was bestowed far more often in Scotland than in any other English-speaking country. It had been popular in England and America in the nineteenth century, though it was never quite popular enough to become one of the

top twenty girls' names. In Scotland, by contrast, Grace
was in 17th position in 1858, and still in 22nd position in
1935. Only then did it begin to fade, dropping to 70th
place by 1958. A 1975 count shows no trace of the name.
Grace was introduced by the Puritans in the seventeenth
century, along with other abstract virtue names such as
Faith, Hope, Charity, Patience, all of which are now
little used. Helena Swan *(Girls' Christian Names)* quotes
Charles Lamb on the subject of 'saying grace,' and comments that 'the Puritan Fathers thought that there were
other things to be grateful for besides food, and tried to
show it in their daughters' names.'

Grace Darling's famous rescue of the Forfarshire sur-
vivors helped make the name popular in all parts of Britain
in the nineteenth century.

Graham (m)   Also **Graeme, Grahame.** This is another
famous Scottish clan name used as a Christian name. The
name has recurred constantly in Scottish history since
William de Graham received from David I the lands of
Abercorn and Dalkeith in the twelfth century. The original
placename Graham may have been 'Granta's homestead'
or 'gravelly homestead.' 'Grey homestead' has also been
suggested, but is unlikely. Graham (excluding other
spellings) was 24th most frequently used name in Scotland
in 1958. It had risen from 56th position in 1935, and there
is no doubt that the rise continued into the 1970's, for the
name is still being intensively used. The spelling *Graeme,*
used by William Buchanan in an eighteenth-century
genealogical work, has also been gaining ground. In 1958,
531 Scottish boys received the name Graham, while 260
became Graeme. Both spellings are now used in equal
numbers. In the 1950's Graham suddenly became a
fashionable name in England and Wales, but it proved to
be a passing fad. Graeme does not seem to have been used
outside Scotland.

Grant (m)　Grant was a well-known Norman nickname for someone who was 'tall.' As a surname *Grant* has been established in Scotland at least since 1263, when Sir Laurence Grant was Sheriff of Inverness. The use of Grant as a Christian name, however, is much more modern, and seems to have begun in North America. In Canada, for example, it was certainly more densely used in the 1950's than in Scotland itself. American usage of the Christian name, never very intensive, may have begun in honour of President Ulysses Grant (1822-85). In the late 1970's Grant has been used quietly by Scottish parents.

Gregor (m)　Also **Gregory, Grigor.** Gaelic **Griogair.** A popular Christian name in early times because of St Gregory (*c.* 540-604), whose name derived from a Greek word meaning 'watchful.' Many Scottish surnames, ranging from *Greer* to *Macgregor,* testify to the frequency of the name's use in Scotland in the Middle Ages, but it has been surprisingly little used in modern times. As Gregory, it has, by contrast, been very popular in North America and Australia. Gregory has also been rapidly coming into fashion in England and Wales since 1965.

Griselda (f)　Also **Grizel, Grizzel, Grissel, Grissell.** A Germanic name of uncertain origin, fairly popular in Scotland in the eighteenth century and before. The latest edition of *The Oxford Dictionary of English Christian Names* (1977) says that 'it is still quite common in Scotland,' but the various reports of the Scottish Registrar General make it quite clear that the name has hardly been used in Scotland since at least 1858.

Chaucer told the story of 'patient Griselda' in *The Clerk's Tale.* His source was Boccaccio, who took it from Petrarch. Griselda's husband tried his wife's patience in various ways, including taking her children from her to be brought up by foster-parents—having told Griselda that he had killed them. Later he brought home a beautiful young lady and said that he intended to divorce Griselda in order to marry the newcomer. Griselda made no murmur of protest, and only then did her husband reveal that the 'rival' was their own daughter. The story was seen in earlier times as a splendid example of the way a wife and mother should behave.

Guy (m)   This was formerly a common Christian name, introduced to Britain by the Normans. It often appeared as **Guido** or **Wido.** Its ultimate etymology is obscure, but it probably derives from a word meaning 'wood.' Guy Fawkes (1570-1606) 'killed' the name in England, nor was it especially common in Scotland after the seventeenth century. Sir Walter Scott's novel *Guy Mannering* (1815) did much to restore its image, and it is currently in quiet but regular use throughout Britain. The American use of the word 'guy' dates only from the end of the nineteenth century. In expressions like 'you guys' it now includes both men and women.

H

Halbert (m)   A Scottish surname occasionally used as a Christian name. It was formerly more common, which has led some experts to suggest that it may be a form of **Albert.** However, Professor Weekley saw this name as derived from the halberd, a long-shafted axe-like weapon with a hook on the back. Miss Yonge seems to have connected it with Scandinavian names such as Norwegian **Hallbjorg** and **Hallbjorn,** where *Hall-* means '(precious) stone,' *-bjorg* is 'help,' and *-bjorn* is 'bear.' Halbert is also listed in a reliable Dutch dictionary of Christian names *(Woordenboek Van Voornamen)* and explained as Germanic, with the meaning 'shining man.' Probably a combination of these various sources gave rise to the name. The pet forms **Hab, Habbie, Hob** and **Hobbie** are recorded.

Hamilton (m)   A noble Scottish surname established since the fourteenth century. It derives from a placename which probably meant 'scarred hill.' It is occasionally used as a male Christian name.

Hamish (m)   A phonetic rendering of Gaelic **Seumas, 'James,'** used in the vocative case, i.e. **Sheumais.** Hamish was 78th most frequently used name in Scotland in 1958, but it seems to have dropped out of favour since then.

Harold (m)   Gaelic **Harailt.** A Norse and Old English name composed of elements meaning 'army' and 'power, rule.' The name was frequently used in Britain at the turn of the century, but it was out of fashion by 1935. In that year it ranked 79th in Scotland, and it was clearly declining fast.

Harry (m)   The pet form of **Henry,** representing the earlier (French) pronunciation of that name. Harry became popular as an independent name in England and Wales at the end of the nineteenth century, eventually going out of favour around 1930. It seems to have come to Scotland much later, reaching a minor peak of popularity in the 1950's. It is now out of fashion. The feminine form is **Harriet** (pet forms **Hatty, Harty**) which was most used in Scotland in the nineteenth century.

Hazel (f)   This tree name began to be used as a Christian name in Scotland in the 1930's. By 1958 it was the 67th most frequently used girls' name. It has been used in the 1970's, but it is clearly past its peak. In England and Wales the name was first used at the end of the nineteenth century, but it only became really popular in the 1960's.

Heather (f)   First used as a Christian name in England and Wales in the 1880's, but at its most popular there

in the 1950's. For obvious reasons the name made a great
appeal to Scottish parents. By 1958 it was 34th most
frequently used name in Scotland, and it has continued
to be used frequently in the late 1970's. The name is no
longer fashionable in England, but it has recently reached
the U.S.A., Canada and Australia, and is establishing itself
firmly. The Latin name for heather is *erica*, which occurs
as a Christian name, but normally as a feminine form of
Eric.

Hector (m)   This famous Greek name probably means
'prop' or 'stay.' It was first used in Scotland as a substitute, or anglicisation, of the Gaelic **Eachd(h)onn,** later
Eachann. Hector was actually the 68th most frequently
used name in Scotland in 1935, which put it above more
obviously Scottish names such as **Hamish, Ewen, Finlay,
Bruce, Dugald,** etc.

Helen (f)   The name of this famous Greek beauty,
renowned in literature, has long been a favourite with
Scottish parents. The name itself derives from a word
meaning 'bright' or 'light,' and it occurs in many forms—
Elaine, Ellen, Elanor, Elinor, etc. **Eileen** and **Aileen**
have also been associated with it.

Helen was the 10th most frequently used girls' name in
Scotland in 1858, and in 8th position in 1958. A count
made in 1975 reveals that it may at last be going out of
fashion, a fate which has already befallen it in the U.S.A.
and Canada. The name there also enjoyed at least a hundred
years of intensive usage, but in the 1950's it was largely
replaced by Ellen. In England and Wales the reverse
happened, with Helen coming into fashion in 1970 to oust
Ellen. Helen is still more popular in England and Wales
than anywhere else in the English-speaking world, though
Scottish parents have not completely deserted it. The
Latin **Helena** (with **Lena** as its pet form) and French
Helene occasionally occur in Scotland. The diminutive

Nellie is sometimes found as an independent name. The Gaelic form of the name is **Eilidh,** and this too is used in Scotland.

Henrietta (f) The feminine form of **Henry** which has never been especially popular in England and Wales. It has been more popular in Scotland, where it was the 82nd most frequently used name in 1935. It was still in use in 1958, but it is now very rarely given. The pet forms **Hetty** and **Etta** have sometimes been used as independent names. Helena Swan, in her *Girls' Christian Names,* also gives **Detta** as a diminutive of Henrietta, and **Henny** is occasionally used.

Henry (m) Gaelic **Eanruig.** A Germanic name composed of elements which mean 'house' and 'ruler.' It was very popular throughout Britain and North America in the nineteenth century, eventually going out of fashion in England and Wales by 1935. The name survived in Scotland until the early 1960's. It was 17th most frequently used name in 1935, 49th in 1958. A count of names given to children born in Scotland in 1975 shows that it is now very rarely used. Some of the surnames that derive from the name, *Henderson, Hendry,* etc., are used occasionally as Christian names. The feminine form of the name is **Henrietta.**

Herbert (m) A Germanic name composed of elements meaning 'army' and 'bright.' It was popular throughout Britain from 1875-1925. By 1935 it was in 86th position in Scotland, and it is now very rarely used.

Hercules (m) The name used in Shetland as a substitute for the Scandinavian **Hakon.** Hercules is the Latin form of Greek **Heracles,** a name meaning 'hera's glory.' **Hera,** 'protectress,' was the mother of Hercules in ancient Greek legend. The Scandinavian name Hakon means 'high offspring.' It also appears as **Hogen,** which is closer to its pronunciation in modern Norway. Men bearing the name Hercules in the Shetlands were known by the pet form **Hakki.**

Hilary (f)   Also **Hilarie, Hillary.** This has been mainly used for girls, very occasionally for boys. It began, in fact, as a male name, meaning 'hilarity, cheerfulness.' As a girls' name it was reasonably well used in Scotland during the 1950's.

Hilda (f)   A Germanic name, probably the first element of compound names in most cases, though occurring as the final element in names like **Mathilda.** It means 'battle.' Hilda was very fashionable in England and Wales from 1900-25. In Scotland it was 90th most frequently used name in 1935, but it was by then clearly going out of fashion. Scott had earlier told the story of St Hilda in *Marmion* (1808). **Hylda** is occasionally found as a variant.

Hugh (m)   Also (rarely) **Hew.** This was used in Scotland as a substitute for several Gaelic names, such as **Uisdean, Eoghan, Aodh,** because of vague similarities in pronunciation. Hugh is actually Germanic in origin, from a root word meaning 'heart, mind.'

In terms of modern usage, Hugh is decidedly Scottish. It was in 12th position in 1858, 15th in 1935, and 28th in 1958. It has recently tended to slip still further down the scale, which seems a pity. The name has hardly been used in other English-speaking countries, except Ireland, during the last hundred years.

In Scotland **Hughina** is occasionally found as a girls' name. There are also many Scottish surnames derived from Hugh or Hew. These include *Hewat, Hewet, Hewit, Hewatson, Hewison, Howat, Howatson, Hugan, Huggin, Hughson,* etc.

Humphrey (m)   A popular Norman name, 'noble and knightly' as Charlotte Yonge described it. It occurs in various clan histories, e.g., Humphrey de Kilpatrick was the founder of the family of *Colquhoun*. It is now little used. The original meaning of the name is obscure, though the second element is 'peace.' The Orkney and Shetland surname *Umphray* or *Umphrey* derives from it. **Humphray** is also found. Early Scots forms of the Christian name include **Umfried, Umfra** and **Aumfray.**

Hunter (m)   This surname (which ranked 32nd in Scotland in 1976) derives from the activity or occupation. It is sometimes used as a Christian name in Scotland.

Huntly (m)   Huntly in Aberdeenshire derived its name from a hamlet in Berwickshire, now extinct. The earls of Huntly took the name northwards. The original meaning of the placename was 'hunting ley or meadow.' Huntly is now occasionally used as a Scottish Christian name.

I

Ian (m)   Also **Iain,** which is the more 'correct' Gaelic form of **John.** There was no sign of Ian or Iain in the Scottish Registrar General's Report of 1858, but by 1935 Ian/Iain was the 10th most frequently used name in Scotland. In 1958 Ian was in 8th place, Iain in 29th. Both forms have continued to be much used by Scottish parents in the late 1970's, with Iain occurring almost as frequently as Ian. Iain may well become the distinctive Scottish form of a name that will be used throughout the rest of the English-speaking world as Ian. The shorter form is already used in great numbers in England, Canada and Australia. American parents have not yet discovered it, but will no doubt do so.

Ina (f)   The pet form of various names ending in -ina, such as **Christina, Georgina.** It is occasionally used in Scotland as a name in its own right. It can be pronounced as *Eena* or *Eye-na*, as the bearer prefers. H. E. Bates has a story called *The Landlady* in which there is the rather extraordinary comment: 'Ina: classy name, too classy.'

Inga (f)   One of the Scandinavian names used in the Shetlands and still kept alive by Scottish parents. It is a short form of many other names, including **Ingeborg, Ingegard** and **Ingrid.** It derives ultimately from the name of an Icelandic god, **Yngvi.** Ingrid ('Yngvi' and 'beauty') is also used in Scotland, but in this case the fame of the Swedish actress Ingrid Bergman (1917-   ) probably has more influence than traditional ties with Scandinavia.

Innes (m, f)   The name of an island (the word means 'island' in Gaelic) which became a Scottish surname, and later a clan name. It is used occasionally in Scotland as a Christian name, normally for boys but also for girls. As a girls' name it comes close in sound to **Inez,** the Spanish form of **Agnes.** The surname *MacInnes,* 'son of Angus,' is not etymologically related.

Iona (f)   The name of this famous Hebridean island, where St Columba founded his monastery in 563, is used from time to time as a girls' Christian name. Ivor Brown remarks perceptively in his *Charm of Names :* 'the smaller islands have been taken up for Christian names on their merits of appearance when one sees them and of music when one hears them.'

Irene (f)   Greek, 'peace.' Very popular in Scotland this century: it was the 18th most frequently used name in 1935, 23rd in 1958, but fading away after 1960. The three-syllable pronunciation is considered to be more correct by the classicists, but *I-reen* was introduced to Britain by means of a successful American musical and has thoroughly established itself. The name was immensely popular in England and Wales around 1925. **Irena** is occasionally used.

Iris (f)   To the Greeks Iris was the goddess of rain, the personification of the 'rainbow,' which is the original meaning of the name. In Britain, Iris was part of the craze for flower names as Christian names which was most noticeable around the turn of the century. Scottish parents made the name 84th most frequently used in 1935, but it is now rarely given.

Irvine (m)   Also **Irvin, Irving.** These are Scottish surnames, deriving from placenames, which are in occasional use as Christian names.

Isabella (f)   The Italian form of **Elizabeth,** and the preferred spelling of a name much used in Scotland until the 1960's. It also occurs as **Isobel, Isobell, Isobella, Isobelle, Isabel** (the modern Spanish form), **Isabell, Isabelle, Ishbel** (Scottish form), **Iseabail** (Gaelic).
  Until the sixteenth century Isabel was used in Britain interchangeably with Elizabeth, a woman so-called using either form of the name at will. As a separate name, Isabella was the 7th most frequently used girls' name in Scotland in 1858, and 6th in 1935. By 1958 it had dropped to 41st place, but its various other forms were also in use. The usual pet forms of the name are **Bel, Bell, Bella, Belle, Ella, Ib, Ibbie, Ibby, Isa, Sib, Tib, Tibbie, Tibby.** Of these, Bella, Ella and Isa were still being used as independent names in Scotland in 1958.

Isla (f)   The name of two Scottish rivers, and one given to 12 girls born in Scotland in 1958. **Islay,** the island name, also occurs, usually as a female Christian name but sometimes male, especially amongst the *Campbells.*

Ismay (f)   Apparently a blend of **Christine** and **Mary** via **Chris** and **May.** A correspondent, Mrs Joan Stewart, of Harris, reports on the use of both first and middle names as an ordinary term of address in the Western Isles. The two names are then likely to take on a shortened, blended form. See also **Chrisselle.**

Ivor (m)   Gaelic **Iomhair.** The Norse personal name **Ivarr** was formerly used in Scotland, leading to surnames such as *MacIver, MacIvor, Maccure.* As the late Ivor Brown, a well-known student of words and names, ex-pressed it: 'My native county of Aberdeenshire once had a share in the strong Scandinavian linguistic infiltration which has had a permanent influence on the customs and vo-cabulary of the Orkney and Shetland islands.' Günther Drosdowski connects the Norse *Ivarr* with **Ingvar,** which contains the name of a god of unknown etymology. The regular occurrence in Ayrshire of the male name **Ivey, Ivie** or **Ivy** is probably originally connected with a pet form of Ivor.

J

Jacqueline (f)   Also **Jackaleen, Jackalene, Jackaline, Jackalyn, Jacolyn, Jacqualine, Jacquelene, Jacquelyn.** Originally a French feminine form of **Jacques (Jacob, James).** In modern times Jacqueline has swept through North America (1920-40) and England and Wales (1945-65). Unknown in Scotland in 1935, Jacqueline became the 12th most frequently used girls' name in 1958. Since then its extreme popularity has led to its downfall, and it has rapidly dropped out of fashion in the late 1970's.

James (m)   From a Hebrew word of uncertain meaning, which developed into Latin **Jacobus** or **Jacomus,** or

Jacob and **James.** In the English translation of the Bible Jacob was used as the name of Isaac's son, while James was used for the Apostles. In Scotland Jacob is rarely used, whereas James has long been outstandingly popular. James has many historical associations in Scotland, especially as a name of Scotland's kings. In 1858 it was being used very nearly as often as **John.** In 1958 James again ran second to John: 4780 Scottish Johns were named that year, and 4181 boys were called James. This means that one boy in ten became John, one in twelve James. The Gaelic vocative form of the name, **Hamish** (from **Seamus),** was also used in 1958. The diminutive forms include **Jim, Jamie** and **Jaime** (occurring as independent names), and **Jem, Jemmy. Jimmy** is also used in Glasgow, especially as a vocative to a stranger. A survey of name usage in 1975 indicates that James has now probably overtaken John in Scotland, but both names have lost considerable ground.

Jamesina (f)   A feminine form of **James** used in Scotland, usually pronounced *Eye-na* rather than *Eena*. In *Georgy Girl*, a novel by Margaret Forster, occurs the passage: 'he couldn't call a girl **Jamesa** or even **Jamesina.** It sounded heathen.' In recent times, especially since the arrival on British television screens of *The Bionic Woman, alias* **Jaime** Somers, Jaime and **Jamie** have been used far more frequently as feminine forms of James. **Jacobina** is another feminine form of James which is occasionally used in Scotland.

Jane (f)   A feminine form of **John** which has had a long run of popularity in Scotland. It was the 5th most frequently used girls' name in 1858, 13th in 1935, 18th in 1958. Since then the downward trend has continued. The Gaelic version is **Sine,** but this is often rendered phonetically as **Sheena, Sheenagh, Sheenah, Shena, Sheona**

or **Shiona.** The spelling **Jayne** is now not unusual, and **Jaine** is an occasional variant.

Janet, Janette (f)   Gaelic **Seònaid.** Diminutives of **Jane. Janetta** is also used occasionally. The fortunes of Janet and Jane have followed the same path in Scotland since 1858. Janet was in 6th position in that year, with Jane 5th. In 1958 Jane was 18th, Janet 19th. However, if the Janes, Jaynes, etc., were counted together as if bearing the same name, and the Janets, Janettes were also considered together, Janet would be the more popular of the two. Janet, which often occurred in former times as **Jonet,** is a decidedly Scottish name in terms of long-established usage. In the 1950's, however, it was intensively used in nearly every other English-speaking country, especially England. *Janette*, stressed on the second syllable in imitation of French **Jeannette,** became at that time temporarily more 'Scottish.' More genuinely Scottish, perhaps, are the pet forms **Jess, Jessie, Jessy, Jennie** and **Jenny, Netta** and **Nita,** all of which occur occasionally as independent names.

Janice (f)   This variant form of **Jane** was first used in Britain in the early 1930's. It seems to have been imported from the U.S.A., where it is recorded as occurring regularly amongst university students who graduated in 1950 at the age of twenty-two. Most 'invented' names emanating from the U.S.A. began with black Americans, but there is no evidence of such an origin in the case of Janice. There is no mention of the name in *Black Names In America*, by Murray Heller, which lists the names of many thousands of black American students. Another American name book, *What To Name Your Baby* (Nurnberg and Rosenblum), mentions a novel 'once widely read' called *Janice Meredith*, by Paul Leicester Ford. It was published in 1899. This seems to be the earliest reference to the name, which does not appear to exist in any other language. In Scotland the spelling **Janis** is sometimes found. **Janyce** and **Jannice** are rarer variants. Janice was the 24th most frequently used name in Scotland in 1958, and it was still being reasonably well used in 1975. Its apparent popularity in the 1950's may have been influenced by the film star, Janice Rule.

Jason (m)   The original meaning of this ancient name is not known, though the *Temple Dictionary of the Bible* suggests that it is a form of **Joshua,** which is itself an alternative form of **Jesus.** Until the 1960's Jason was a well-known but very rarely used Christian name in the English-speaking world. That situation changed drastically within a few years, turning the name, as if overnight, into one of the most frequently given names. The name is still being intensively used in Scotland, but there has been a strong reaction against it by some parents, partly because of the frequency with which it occurs, partly because it has been associated with various television characters.

Jean (f)   A feminine form of **John,** long popular in Scotland. It was the 14th most frequently used name in 1858, 8th in 1935, 21st in 1958. Since then it appears to have fallen out of favour. Between 1925 and 1950 the name became immensely popular in the U.S.A. and Canada, and also in England and Wales. The diminutive **Jeanie** is often used as an independent name. **Jeanna, Jeanne** and **Jeannie** also occur. The Gaelic form is **Sine** (see **Jane**).

Jeanette (f)   The usual Scottish spelling of French **Jeannette,** a diminutive of **Jeanne,** itself the feminine of **Jean** (the French equivalent to **John**). Jeanette was fairly well used by Scottish parents in the 1950's but it is now out of fashion.

Jemima (f)   Hebrew, 'dove.' This was the name of one of
Job's daughters, and its occurrence in the Old Testament
sanctioned its use amongst the Puritans. It was reasonably
popular in Scotland in the nineteenth century, and in 1858
it was the 25th most frequently used name for girls. In
1935 it was still in 61st position, but only 23 girls born in
Scotland received the name in 1958. Miss E. G. Withycombe
may have had something to do with this by referring to
Jemima in her dictionary as 'an ugly name.' Sir Walter
Scott used the name for a character in his story, *My Aunt
Margaret's Mirror*. A pet form was **Mima.** The Gaelic form
was **Simeag.**

Jennifer (f)   Occasionally **Jenifer,** which is the earlier
Cornish spelling. In parish registers of the seventeenth
and eighteenth centuries the name also occurs as **Gweniver,**
which hints at its connection with the name of King
Arthur's wife, Welsh **Gwenhwyfar,** Norman **Guinevere.**
The original meaning of the name has to do with 'white-
ness, fairness' and 'smooth, yielding.'

Jennifer was at one time a purely Cornish name. It
spread into the rest of England after 1925, becoming
highly popular in 1950. Scottish parents made it their
50th most frequently used name in 1958, and used it more
and more in the years that followed. It has only just
showed signs of fading away in the late 1970's. Meanwhile
the name 'arrived' in the U.S.A. and Canada, where it
was top name in 1975. The short forms **Jenny** and **Jennie**
sometimes occur as independent names, though in Scotland
these are traditionally more closely associated with **Janet.**

Jessie (f)   Gaelic **Seasaidh.** In Scotland this is the
diminutive of **Janet,** though elsewhere the name would be
associated with **Jessica.** Compare Scottish **Maisie** for
Margaret. Jessie has been much celebrated in Scottish
poetry. Robert Tannahill (1774-1811), the Paisley poet,
wrote of Janet Tennant as 'charming young Jessie, the

flow'r o' Dunblane,' while Burns wrote of the 'grace, beauty and elegance,' which kept Jessie's lover by her side. In the nineteenth century this form of the name was almost as popular in Scotland as Janet itself. Jessie was the 12th most frequently used name in 1858, 14th in 1935. By 1958, however, it had dropped dramatically to 97th place. The use of Jessie to describe an effeminate man presumably contributed to its downfall.

Joan (f)   Gaelic **Seonag**. Another feminine form of **John**, less popular in Scotland than **Jane** or **Jean**. The name was often spelt **Johan** in the early part of this century, and pronounced as two syllables. This spelling is still occasionally used, together with **Johann, Johanna, Johanne**. Joan swept through the English-speaking world in the 1920's, remaining very popular for thirty years. In the 1970's it has tended to be replaced by **Joanne, Joanna, Jo-ann,** etc.

John (m)   Hebrew, 'God is gracious.' It has been said, in partial explanation of this name's great popularity, that the name of John the Baptist was considered particularly suitable for the baptismal ceremony. John was Scotland's most frequently given name for centuries, but it has begun to lose ground. There has been a certain amount of reaction against it since 1960 in all English-speaking countries, though perhaps it is the habit of naming sons after male relations that is changing. As the use of John diminishes, its other forms, such as **Ian, Sean,** etc., become more popular. **Jonathan** is looked upon by many parents as a more fanciful form of John, although it is in fact a separate name. Johns are still called **Jack** or **Jock** in Glasgow and elsewhere. Jack is also often given as an independent name. Many bearers of the name John have preferred to spell it **Jon** in the late 1970's. See also **Ian**.

Jonathan(m)   Hebrew, 'Jehovah has given.' This has been used in recent years as if it were a fanciful variation of **John.** It was previously little used in Scotland. In the Highlands it is used as the equivalent of **Eoin,** John being used for **Iain.**

Joseph (m)   Hebrew, 'Jehovah increases.' A very great favourite in Scotland until recent times. The name was in 18th position in 1858, 13th in 1935, 23rd in 1958. Subsequently it fell out of fashion. In England and Wales the name has been little used since 1930.

Josephine (f)   This feminine form of **Joseph** is a Scottish and Irish name by use. In Scotland it was most used in the early part of the century. The 1935 name count put it in 57th position; by 1958 it had fallen to 80th place. It is still being used, but not in great numbers. **Josepha** is an occasional variant. The pet forms include **Jo** and **Josie.**

Joyce (f)   'A curious name,' according to Mrs Henry Wood, writing in 1861. In the 1920's, however, it became one of the most popular Christian names in Britain. In Scotland it was 37th most frequently used name in 1935 and it held the same position in 1958. Its diminutive **Joy** was also being used during that period. The original name appears to have been male, that of a Breton saint, **Jodocus** or **Josse,** but William Camden *(Remains Concerning Britain)* listed it in 1605 as a woman's name, deriving it from Latin *jocosa,* 'merry.' Ben Jonson had a female character called Joyce, a servant girl, in his *Tale of a Tub* (1633). Perhaps because of its lower-class associations, Joyce seems to have faded from use until its revival this century.

Judith (f)   Hebrew, 'a Jewess.' The male version of the name has been made world-famous by **Yehudi** Menuhin. Judith was formerly a distinctively Jewish name, but it had a run of general popularity, in Scotland as elsewhere in Britain, in the 1950's.

Julia, Julie (f)   Gaelic **Sileas.** Julie has been the more usual form of this name in Scotland in recent times. Both Julia and Julie are feminine forms of **Julius,** a Roman clan name said to mean 'downy,' or as Camden *(Remains Concerning Britain)* translated it, 'mossy bearded.' Julie is currently very much in fashion in Scotland. The diminutives **Juliet, Juliette** and **Julienne** are occasionally used. The male form of the name, **Julian,** seems to be little used in Scotland.

June (f)   Like **April,** this month name was first used in Britain as a Christian name in the 1920's. The idea seems to have been imported from France, where **Avril** was being used (French 'April'). June was 35th most frequently used name in Scotland in 1935, 31st in 1958. It is now little used. Month names have been more used in Scotland this century than in any other English-speaking country. The existence of **May,** as a pet form of names such as **Mary** rather than the name of the month, may have had some influence.

K

Kara (f)   This is probably a pet form of **Karen,** which is itself a form of **Katharine.** It is fast becoming popular in the U.S.A. (e.g. as the name of Senator Edward Kennedy's only daughter) and it is spreading to other English-speaking countries, including Scotland. Gaelic speakers may link it with **Farquhar** and interpret it as 'friend.' The name is considered to be 'Irish' in Boston, according to Frank Thompson, an American observer of name usage. Bostonian pronunciation links it with **Kieran,**

though the two names are not related etymologically.
See also **Cara.**

Karen (f) A Scandinavian form of **Katrine,** or
Katharine. Another spelling (the more usual one in
Scandinavian countries) is **Karin.** This is occasionally
used in Scotland. Karen was almost unknown in the
English-speaking world until the late 1930's, yet by 1950
it was amongst the top ten names being given to girls born
in the U.S.A. In 1958 it was in 4th position in England
and Wales, becoming top name in 1960; though it has
begun to fade away since 1970. In Scotland the name was
in 30th position in 1958 and subsequently climbed much
higher. An unofficial count made in 1975 showed that it was
still one of the most frequently used names in Scotland.

Kay (f) Also **Kaye.** There was a slight flurry of interest
in this name around 1960. It abbreviates, and to some
extent depersonalises, various other names beginning with
K-.

Keir (m) This Scottish surname, occasionally used as a
Christian name, derives either from a placename or from
the Gaelic personal name based on *ciar*, 'swarthy, dusky.'

Keith (m) A Scottish placename which became a surname, then a Christian name. It was most used as such in
the 1950's, being in 43rd position in Scotland in 1958. The
name was certainly not confined to Scotland, but was used
in great numbers in all English-speaking countries.
English and Welsh parents began to use it in the 1920's,
and by 1950 it was ranked 18th. In North America Keith
arrived rather later and is still being well used. It also
continues to please Scottish and Irish parents, but elsewhere
it has fallen out of fashion.

Kelvin (m)   The name of this Scottish river (of uncertain origin) is occasionally used as a Christian name by Scottish parents.

Kennedy (m)   Gaelic **Ceannaideach,** 'ugly headed,' but the Highland *Kennedys* are known as *MacUalraig,* 'son of **Ulrick.**' This surname was established in Scotland by the twelfth century and spread throughout the country. Kennedy is used quietly but consistently as a Scottish Christian name.

Kenneth (m)   A Scottish name by origin and usage. Kenneth MacAlpine (died *c.* 860), first king of Scotland, was probably named in honour of St **Cainnech,** whose name is preserved in the surname *MacKenzie.* The name anglicises two Gaelic forms, **Coinneach** 'fair one' and **'Cinaed** 'firesprung.' Kenneth was 32nd most frequently used name in Scotland in 1858, and it was at that time almost uniquely Scottish. By 1935 it was in 27th place in Scotland, but it had by then spread to all English-speaking countries and become a great favourite. The name is once again Scottish: Scottish parents have remained faithful to it while parents in other English-speaking countries have now left it aside. **Kenna** is sometimes used as a feminine form, as is **Kennethina** *(Eye-na)*. This can be shortened in the Highlands to **Kennag** (pronounced *Kenn-ac*), spelt **Ceanag** in Gaelic.

Kentigern (m)   The name of Glasgow's patron saint and sixth-century bishop was used as a Christian name in that area mainly in the sixteenth and seventeenth centuries. It often took the form **Quintigern.** The name's original meaning was possibly 'chief lord.' See also **Mungo.**

Kerr (m)   A famous Scottish surname, which often occurs
in the history of Border warfare. It is derived from a placename, which in turn meant 'brushwood.' **Ker** and **Carr**
are alternative spellings of the surname, which is also used
as a Christian name.

Kerry (f)   Also **Keri, Kerrie.** Very much a name of the
1970's in Scotland. In spite of its obvious associations
with Ireland (the county of Kerry originally being that of
Ciar's people), Kerry seems to have come from Australia.
As **Kerrie** it was already being intensively used there in the
1940's, at first both for girls and boys. Subsequently it
became a girls' name only. Presumably the name was
first used as a conscious borrowing from the Irish placename, but a phonetic confusion with **Carrie,** the pet form
of **Caroline,** etc., has been suggested.

Kevin (m)   Occasionally **Kevan,** which is a Scottish surname. Kevin is normally thought of as Irish, since it has
long been a favourite with Irish parents. Its use there
seems to be in honour of several Irish saints named
Caoimhghin, 'comely birth.' Kevin became popular in
most English-speaking countries in the 1960's. In Scotland
it was 53rd most frequently used name in 1958. Since
then it has become rather more popular.

Kim (f)   A shortened form of **Kimberley** or **Kimberly,**
though Rudyard Kipling's Kim was properly **Kimball**
O'Hara. There are several places in England called
Kimberley, probably containing Old English personal
names such as **Cyneburg** or **Cynebald.** The -ley in the
name is a common element in placenames and has many
possible original meanings, but the general sense of the name
was 'land belonging to Cyneburg (or Cynebald).' The
placename early became a surname, and in the nineteenth

century one family still bearing it was that of the English colonial secretary, Lord Kimberley. Kimberley, in South Africa, was named in his honour in 1870. This town became well-known in the Boer War, and in 1900 the sons of many British soldiers were named Kimberley in commemoration of the battle that took place there.

As a male Christian name Kimberley then disappeared, to re-surface as a girls' name in the 1950's, especially in the U.S.A. and Canada. Actresses such as Kim Stanley, Kim Novak and Kim Hunter all helped the name along at that time. Some American parents expanded it to **Kimberly,** conforming to American spelling. There are in fact places bearing that form of the name in Idaho and Montana. In Britain it was also expanded by some parents, who wavered between Kimberly or Kimberley. (**Beverly/ Beverley** is a similar American/British pair of names). In Scotland in 1958, 97 girls were named Kim, 3 became Kimberley, and 3 more Kimberly. There were also 3 Scottish boys named Kim that year, and one other who was named **Kym.** As a girls' name Kim has continued to be used in Scotland since 1958, but it is slowly going out of use.

Kirk (m)　This Christian name looks Scottish, but it has been used far more in America and Canada than in Scotland. The word itself derives from the Norse for 'church,' and it was residence near a church that led to *Kirk* as a surname. Christian-name usage may have begun with a transferred use of the surname. Kirk was certainly being used as a Christian name in the U.S.A. by 1940. In 1941 Issur Danielovitch Demsky began his acting career and changed his name to Kirk Douglas—'Douglas' was in honour of the film star, Douglas Fairbanks Junior; 'Kirk' was chosen because it sounded 'snazzy.' The increased use of the Christian name that occurred in the 1950's was undoubtedly directly due to Kirk Douglas's film career.

L

Lachlan (m) Gaelic **Lachunn, Lachlann.** Lachlan is preserved in the clan name *Maclachlan*. Professor A. Bugge argues that this name means 'Norway, fjord-land.' As a Christian name in Scotland it ranked 35th in 1858 and 92nd in 1935. The name seems to be unknown in other English-speaking countries. A **Lachlanina** was named in Scotland in 1958.

Laura (f) Until the 1960's, this name was far more popular in the U.S.A. and Canada than in Britain. However, since then it has taken hold in England, Wales and Scotland. It is clearly set to go on rising in popularity.

The affection for Laura (a feminine form of **Laurence**) in North America has led to a whole host of adaptations, many of which are now used in Scotland. They include such names as **Laraine, Larraine, Lauraine, Lauranne, Laureen, Lauren, Laurene, Laurie, Laurina, Laurine, Lora, Loraine, Lorana, Loreen, Loren, Lorena, Lorene, Loretta, Lorraine, Lorretta, Lorriane, Lauretta, Laurana, Laureola, Laurel, Lori, Lorelle,** etc. One or two are independent names from other sources, e.g., Lorraine and Laurel, but the names as a whole indicate a liking for the initial sound contained in them.

Some of these forms are far older than one might think. For instance, Sheridan was already poking gentle fun at Lauretta in the eighteenth century. One of the characters in his play *St Patrick's Day* (1775) holds forth about the effect of names on character:

'Lauretta! aye, you would have her called so; but for my part I never knew any good come of giving girls these heathen Christian names: if you had called her Deborah, or Tabitha, or Ruth, or Rebecca, or Joan, nothing of this had ever happened; but I always knew Lauretta was a runaway name.'

Laurence, Lawrence (m)   Gaelic **Labhruinn.** The spelling *Lawrence* has been slightly preferred in Scotland to *Laurence.* **Laurance** also occurs, as do the pet forms **Larry, Laurie** and **Lawrie,** used as independent names. The origin of all the forms is a Latin name meaning 'someone from the town of Laurentum (in Latium).' The placename may in turn derive from *laurus,* the laurel or bay tree. St Laurence was a third-century martyr, one of the most famous of the city of Rome. His name has been used everywhere in the Christian world, in such forms as the Scandinavian **Lars** or **Lasse,** German **Lorenz,** Italian and Spanish **Lorenzo,** French **Laurent.** In modern times, of the English-speaking countries, the U.S.A. has used the name most, usually as Lawrence. In Britain, Scottish parents have used it most, especially earlier this century. In 1935 the name was the 49th most frequently used in Scotland, but it has tended to fade away since then. Today *Laurence* seems to be the normal spelling, *Lawrence* being reserved for the surname. The medieval popularity of St Laurence in Scotland is reflected in placenames such as Laurencekirk and Lauriston.

Lee (m, f)   This is a surname derived from a common placename which has a variety of original meanings, such as 'wood,' 'clearing,' 'pasture.' In Scotland it is used as a Christian name for both girls and boys, and is no longer thought of as a transferred surname. In England and Wales there is a tendency to spell the girls' name as **Leigh,** perhaps in allusion to the actress Vivien Leigh (1913-67). The use of the name for boys began in the U.S.A., probably in honour of General Robert E. Lee (1807-70).

Lennox (m, f)   This Scottish placename, which is also a surname, is occasionally used as a Christian name for both girls and boys. The original meaning of the placename, according to Mackenzie *(Scottish Place Names),* has to do with 'elm trees.'

Leonard (m) Germanic, 'lion bold.' This name was reasonably popular in Scotland at the beginning of the present century. It was in 70th position in the Scottish lists in 1935, but it is now very rarely used.

Lesley, Leslie (f, m) The Aberdeenshire placename led to the surname and clan name, then to middle-name and first-name usage. The name was in regular but quiet use as a Christian name from the 1840's; by 1875 it was also being used in England and Wales. The feminine form, Lesley, was introduced into general use in the 1880's, though it had been established by Robert Burns in the previous century in his poem *Bonnie Lesley*.

As a boys' name Leslie became fashionable throughout Britain in the 1920's. By 1935 it was 50th most frequently used name in Scotland, and it was still in 56th place in 1958. It has subsequently fallen out of use, possibly because Lesley became far more popular for girls in the early 1950's. Leslie had never been especially popular as a male name in the U.S.A., though it was the original first name of President (Gerald) Ford. When Leslie Caron appeared on the cinema screens in *Gigi* (1958) she instantly brought that form of the name into fashion for girls. The spelling *Lesley* is unknown in the U.S.A. Lesley has been used in Scotland in the late 1970's, but now shows signs of going out of fashion.

Letitia (f) Latin *laetitĩa,* 'gladness.' A very popular name throughout Britain in former times. It usually took the form **Lettice.** This has long been virtually extinct, but Scottish parents have remained relatively faithful to Letitia. By doing so they have almost made it a Scottish name. The pet forms **Lettie** and **Letty** are used.

Lewis (m) Gaelic **Luthais.** Originally this was a form of French **Louis,** German **Ludwig,** but it is now regarded as a separate name with a different pronunciation. The name is composed of elements meaning 'loud' (='famous') and 'battle, war.' In Scotland, however, Lewis is naturally associated with the placename. A correspondent, Mrs Joan Stewart, reports on its use in the Western Isles, but American parents have used the name most in recent times. The name reached its minor peak of popularity in Scotland in the 1930's. The feminine form **Lewise** was used in Scotland in 1958.

Liam (m)   This Irish pet form of **William** is occasionally used as an independent name in Scotland.

Lilian, Lillian (f)   Gaelic **Lileas.** The Scottish forms of the name are **Lilias** or **Lillias,** which appear to link with the name of a Spanish martyr **Liliosa.** The latter name is rendered as **Liliana** in Italian (see Burgio, *Dizionario dei Nomi Propri di Persona*). The origin of all these forms is probably Latin *lilium*, 'lily,' which has long been a symbol of purity. **Susan** also means 'lily' in Hebrew. **Lily,** Gaelic **Lilidh,** has itself been used as a Christian name, especially when flower names were in vogue from 1880 onwards. Lilian/Lillian has been quietly used in Scotland, and is now decidedly unfashionable.

Linda (f)   Linda was used occasionally in Britain throughout the nineteenth century, at that time as a pet form of names such as **Belinda, Malinda, Melinda, Rosalinda,** etc. It came into its own, however, in the 1940's, quickly becoming one of the top names in the English-speaking world. In Scotland it appeared from nowhere to take 4th place in 1958. Only **Margaret, Mary** and **Elizabeth** were able to resist its challenge. The name seems to have been imported from the U.S.A. where it was borne (as a stage name) by actresses such as Linda Darnell and Linda Christian. In Spanish the word *linda* is a feminine form of the word for 'pretty,' which no doubt influenced many American parents. In fact, as an element in much older names, usually Germanic, *linda* or *linde* meant

'serpent,' the serpent being renowned for its wisdom. The
very popularity of Linda has now caused parents everywhere to turn away from it. It is occasionally found as
Lynda, Lynnda or **Lindy.**

Lindsay (m, f) This is the normal form of the Scottish
surname and clan name, which is said to derive from either
a Norman or English placename. Randolph de Lindesay
was the nephew of William the Conqueror and brought
the name to Britain. It has been established in Scotland
since the twelfth century. As a Christian name it has been
surprisingly popular in all English-speaking countries
recently; surprisingly because of the sexual and ortho-
graphic confusion associated with the name. In 1958, for
example, Scottish parents gave the name to their children
as follows: (boys) Lindsay, 63: (girls) Lindsay, 37;
Lindsey, 21; **Linsay,** 21; **Linsey,** 1; **Lyndsay** 12; **Lynd-
saye,** 1; **Lyndsey,** 3; **Lynsay,** 2. A 1975 count in Scotland
shows Lyndsay and **Lynsey** being used, both for girls. The
name seems to have settled down now as a girls' name.

Lisa (f) This form of **Elizabeth** has been brought to
Britain from the U.S.A. It has been extremely well used
in England and Wales since 1965, and it is clearly popular
in the late 1970's with Scottish parents.

Logan (m) A number of places in Scotland bear this name.
Black *(Surnames of Scotland)* thinks that Logan in Ayrshire
gave rise to the surname, which is now in occasional
use as a Christian name. The placename is said to derive
from words meaning 'little hollow.'

Lorna (f) A Lorna was named in England in the
eighteenth century, but R. D. Blackmore probably invented
the name independently for his novel *Lorna Doone* (1869).
Lorna is used far more in Scotland than in other English-
speaking countries, presumably because of the familiarity

of the surname and placename, *Lorne*. A 'Lord Lorne' is mentioned in the novel, but no reason is given for the naming of Lorna, who is eventually revealed to be Lady Lorna *Dugal*. This surname may be significant for the *MacDougalls* of Lorn were once famous.

Lorne (m, f) Lorne was used as both a male and female Christian name by Scottish parents in 1958. **Lorn** has also been used to name Scottish girls. *Lorne* is the usual surname form, while Lorn, in Argyllshire, is the place that gave rise to the name. The original meaning of the placename is obscure.

Lorraine (f) Also **Loraine.** Imported from France in the 1940's and used more in Scotland than elsewhere in the English-speaking world. The name derives from *Jeanne la Lorraine,* '**Joan,** the girl from Lorraine,' or as we know her, Joan of Arc. Jeanne was born at Domremy, Lorraine, in 1411. This province in North-East France was the 'kingdom of *Lothair*' (Latin *Lotharii regnum*). Lothair, which is the same as modern German **Lothar,** originally meant 'famous army,' but there is little doubt that the French parents who first began to use Lorraine as a Christian name were simply thinking of St Joan. By 1958 Lorraine was 27th most frequently used name in Scotland. It would have ranked still higher if the Loraines had been counted with the Lorraines. The name remains very popular in the late 1970's. Some parents no doubt associate it with names like **Laura** and **Lauren.** Others may connect it with the mother of Mary Queen of Scots, who was Mary of Lorraine. *Lorraine, Loraine* and *Lorain* are also Scottish surnames, showing that the original name-bearers came from the French district.

Louise (f) This name was formerly popular in the Latin form, **Louisa,** but it is now more often spelt and pronounced as French *Louise*. Both are feminine forms of

Louis, which is itself rarely used in Scotland, **Lewis** being preferred. Louise has been very much in fashion throughout Britain, including Scotland, in the late 1970's.

Lucy (f) This name is the English form of **Lucia,** feminine of the Latin name **Lucius,** 'light.' A more accurate translation might be 'dawn,' for Lucia and Lucius were used to name children born at day-break. Saint Lucy was a popular saint in the Middle Ages and her name was well used throughout Britain. It faded away in the nineteenth century, perhaps because the Lucys mentioned in literature around that time were not particularly fortunate. Sir Walter Scott made Lucy Ashton the Bride of Lammermoor in his novel of that name. She tries to murder the man she has been forced to marry and dies insane. Lucy has recently come back into fashion in England, and there are signs that Scottish parents are also using it once more. They also use the French form **Lucie,** and diminutives such as **Lucilla, Lucille, Lucinda, Lucetta, Lucette, Lucienne. Lucyna** was also used in Scotland in 1958. The Gaelic form of the name is **Liusaidh.**

Ludovic (m) This was used especially by the *Grants* in former times as a substitute for Gaelic **Maoldomhnaich,** 'Sunday's servant,' i.e., servant of the church. Professor Watson *(History of the Celtic Place-Names of Scotland)* says of the Gaelic name that 'in Skye this name was given to a boy whose maintenance was provided for by the Sunday's collection.' Ludovic is in fact from Latin Ludovicus, the usual English form of which is **Lewis.**

Lulach (m) A name found in Scotland in the eleventh century, probably meaning 'little calf.' It survives in the surname *Maclullich.*

Lyle (m)   A Scottish surname occasionally used as a male
Christian name. It derives from Norman French, and is
the same as *Lisle,* formerly *L'Isle,* 'the island.' Mrs Craik
says in her novel *Olive* (1850): 'She learnt their Christian
names, Robert and Lyle—the latter of which she admired
very much, and thought it exactly suited the pretty, delicate
younger brother.'

Lynn, Lynne (f)   A fashionable modern name element,
as well as a separate name, for traditional names such as
Caroline, Kathleen and **Jacqueline** have all tended to
become **Carolyn, Kathlyn** and **Jacquelyn** in recent
years. The Registrar General's Report for Scotland (1958)
separated the two spellings of the name, thereby placing
Lynn in 51st position, Lynne in 68th position. Counted
together the composite name Lyn(n)(e) was actually as
popular in 1958 as **Lesley** or **Karen.** Both forms of the
name were still being used in Scotland in the late 1970's.
The spelling **Lyn** was also to be found occasionally. The
name will be heard a great deal for many years to come,
since in ordinary speech it is the pet form of names like
Lindsay and **Linda,** as well as a name in its own right.
In former times Lynn and Lynne were used to name boys,
especially in the U.S.A. They are still sometimes used
in this way.

M

Mabel (f)   Originally a pet form of **Amabel,** 'amiable,'
though used in Ireland as an English substitute for
Meadhbh, or **Maeve.** The latter name is more recognisable
as that of the fairy queen, Queen **Mab.**

Mabel was most used in Britain around the turn of the
century. Helena Swan discussed it in her *Girls' Christian
Names* (1900), saying that 'most people when they give their

little children this pretty name probably think that it is a French one, and that it means 'my beautiful one.' Miss Swan was no doubt correct, for the name often appeared as **Mabelle** and was probably normally pronounced as if it were the French expression, *ma belle*. In *A Scots Quair*, by Lewis Grassic Gibbon, there is a reference to a 'quean called Mabel—by all but her mother, she called her May-bull.' The latter pronunciation was formerly the English one and is now standard. The name remained popular until 1920, but it has since been little used. An old form, **Mabella,** is sometimes found in Scotland.

Macdonald (m)   Gaelic **Domhnall.** This famous clan name and surname is quite often used as a Scottish Christian name. It means, of course, 'son of **Donald.**'

Magnus (m)   Latin, 'great.' A name associated with the royal families of Norway and Denmark, imported into Scotland via Shetland. Only 6 boys born in Scotland in 1958 received this name (though a further 6 received it in its Gaelic form, **Manus**). It has probably been more used in Scotland in the late 1970's because of the exposure given to it by the television personality, Magnus Magnusson.

Mairi (f)   The usual spelling in Scotland of the Gaelic form of **Mary,** though the vocative form **Mhairi,** pronounced *Vahri,* also occurs fairly frequently. **Mairie, Mhari, Mharie** and **Mhairie** also occur. The name is pronounced by Gaelic speakers with the stress on the first syllable. Mairi has never been one of the top hundred names in Scotland, but it continues to be used regularly.

Maisie (f)   Originally a pet form of **Margaret.** Since **Daisy** also came to be used as a nickname for Margaret it is tempting to see Maisie as a blend of Margaret and Daisy. However, Maisie was in very early use and its form has

probably more to do with the Gaelic **Marsail, 'Margery.'**
Mysie was another form of the name. As a name in its own
right, Maisie has never been particularly fashionable in any
English-speaking country, though its use increased for a
time *circa* 1925.

Malcolm (m)   From Gaelic **Maol-Caluim,** 'servant or
disciple of St **Columba**.' Malcolm is famous in Scottish
history because of King Malcolm III, called 'Canmore'
(*c.* 1031-93), husband of Queen Margaret. The name was
ranked 24th in Scotland in 1858, but it had dropped
to 42nd place by 1935. In 1958 it was in 44th position,
and there is clear evidence to show that it has since
dropped out of fashion altogether. In England and Wales
Malcolm was taken up for a brief period around 1950,
while in Canada and Australia it has also been reasonably
well used. The Americans have yet to discover the name.
Malcolmina has sometimes been used as a feminine form.

Malise (m)   Gaelic **Maol Iosa,** 'servant of Jesus.' Formerly a favourite name with the *Grahams,* and borne by
several earls of Strathearn. It survives in surname form as
Mellis.

Malvina (f)   Gaelic **Malmhin.** A name from Macpherson's Ossianic poems (1765) which is occasionally used in
Scotland. **Morna,** the name of Fingal's mother in the
same poems, is also used from time to time.

Margaret (f)   Gaelic **Mairead** (**Marghrad** in Lewis).
'The national Scottish female name,' as Charlotte Yonge
rightly called it in her *History of Christian Names* (1863).
Introduced to Scotland from Hungary by Queen Margaret
(*c.* 1046-93), the name has remained an outstanding
favourite until very recent times. In 1975 a sample count
showed that it was still being used intensively in Scotland,
but that it was no longer number one name, a position it

held in 1858, 1935 and 1958. The old habit of naming
children after parents, grandparents and other relations
seems to be breaking down, with the consequent introduction of new names. However, in Scotland in the late
1970's one woman in every eighteen was called Margaret,
irrespective of her age. Also there are many women called
**Margo, Margot, Margarete, Margaretta, Margarette,
Margarita, Marguerita, Marguerite, Greta** and **Rita**,
all of which are closely connected with Margaret. Many
of the name's diminutive forms are also used as independent
names. These include **Margery, Marjorie, Marjory,
Maisie, May, Maggie, Madge, Meta,** and **Peggy.**

The origin of this 'Scottish' name is thought to be Persian,
a word that meant 'pearl.' This accounts for the occasional
use of **Pearl** as a nickname for Margaret. Another
nickname is **Daisy,** because the daisy or marguerite
generally blooms round about St Margaret's Day, February
22nd.

Sir Walter Scott named many of his characters
Margaret, or variants of the name. There is **Mysie** in *The
Bride of Lammermoor* (1819), **Meg** Merrilies in *Guy
Mannering* (1815), Peggy in *Old Mortality* (1816), Maisie
and Margaret in his ballads.

Maria (f)   A popular modern alternative, in Scotland as
elsewhere in the English-speaking world, to **Mary.** Maria
was formerly in vogue when Latinised spellings of names
were felt to be 'correct.' As to the name's pronunciation,
there is an interesting comment by Thackeray in his
Pendennis : (1849): 'Fancy marrying a woman of low rank of
life . . . fancy your wife attached to a woman who
dropped her H's, or called Maria Marire!'

Maria is the Spanish and Italian form of Mary. The
French form of the name, **Marie,** is even more popular
with Scottish parents.

Marie (f)   The French form of **Mary,** and properly

pronounced with the stress on the second syllable. Some speakers equate the name with Gaelic **Mairi** and pronounce it by stressing the first syllable. Marie was 33rd most frequently used name in Scotland in 1858. It had fallen to 72nd position in 1935, but then climbed to 43rd position by 1958. It continues to be well used by Scottish parents in place of Mary.

Marilyn (f)   There was a slight flurry of interest in this variation of **Mary** in the 1950's, when the American film actress, Marilyn Monroe, was receiving a great deal of publicity, but the name has not taken hold in Scotland.

Marion (f)   A diminutive form of **Mary.** The Scottish Registrar General's count placed it in 13th position in 1858, 16th in 1935, 28th in 1958. It has subsequently gone out of fashion. The spelling **Marian** is sometimes used (in 1958 Scottish parents used Marion 450 times, Marian 33 times). Other variants include **Marianne, Marieanne, Mariona, Marrion.** Marion is used by Gaelic speakers as a substitute for **Mor** or **Morag.**

Marisa (f)   Also **Marise, Marissa.** Occasionally used in Scotland, these names are apparently from the Continent, where the custom is to blend such pairs of names as **Maria** and **Elisa** or **Marie Elise.**

Marjorie, Marjory (f)   Also **Margery,** though usage in Scotland in 1958 was as follows: Marjorie, 54; Marjory, 49; Margery, 4. These were originally forms of **Margaret,** but they have long been used as independent names. The Gaelic form is **Marsali.** Marjorie/Marjory was popular in the nineteenth century in Scotland, being 30th most frequently used name in 1858. It was still in 32nd place in 1935, but it subsequently fell out of favour. English and Welsh parents used the name fairly intensively around 1925, but they have since left it aside.

In her novel *Female Friends* Fay Weldon gives a possible reason for the name's demise when she makes a character called Marjorie say: 'I hated margarine. Everyone called me **Marge** at school.'

Mark (m)   The Latin form of this name, **Marcus,** is also occasionally used in Scotland, and the French **Marc** is currently fashionable in most English-speaking countries. The name ultimately relates to the Roman god of war, *Mars*, and is therefore associated with 'martial' activities. Mark came into fashion in the U.S.A. and Canada in the 1940's and has been extremely popular there ever since. The name was also taken up in England and Wales in the 1950's, reaching Scotland a few years later, though the Border *Kerrs* were using the name earlier. By 1958 Mark was the 54th most frequently used name in Scotland, but a count made in 1975 shows that it thereafter became far more popular. It is very much a name of the 1970's. The feminine form **Marcia** is as yet little used in Scotland, though it has been popular in the U.S.A. recently, pronounced—and often spelt—as **Marsha.** The Scottish surname *Mark* probably derives from 'march,' the Borders being formerly divided into East, Middle and West March.

Marlene (f)   In modern times the use of this name has been almost entirely due to Marlene Dietrich (*c*. 1904-   ), and to the wartime song, *Lili Marlene*. Miss Dietrich was born **Maria Magdalena,** and the stage name blended them. However, Charlotte Yonge (*History of Christian Names*) had already listed **Marlena** as a pet form of **Magdalena** in the nineteenth century. Marlene was most used in Scotland in the 1950's. A variant **Marlyn** was also introduced. See also **Arlene.**

Marshall (m)   The surname *Marshall* can indicate either an ancestor who was a farrier, or one who was an officer in the royal household, responsible for important ceremonies.

It is another of the surnames which, in Scotland especially, is regularly used as a Christian name.

Martha (f)   Aramaic, 'the lady.' A reasonably popular name in Scotland in the nineteenth century. It ranked 21st in 1858, 34th in 1935, but it is now rarely used. The name survived far longer in the U.S.A. because of Martha Washington, the first First Lady. It is especially popular with black American parents. The pet forms include **Matty, Mattie** and **Patty.**

Martin (m)   Gaelic **Màrtainn.** A Latin name connected with *Mars,* the god of war, and possibly meaning 'war-like.' The commonness of *Martin* and *MacMartin* as Scottish surnames, together with the name's occurrence in placenames such as Strathmartin and Kilmartin, make it clear that Martin was popular in the Middle Ages. This was due to St Martin of Tours (*c.* 316-97), the founder of monasticism in Gaul. Martin later fell into disuse as a Scottish Christian name but it re-appeared in the 1930's and has steadily risen in popularity since then. The spelling **Martyn** is sometimes used. In England and Wales Martin became especially popular around 1960. The feminine forms of the name are **Martine** and **Martina;** the latter has shown all the signs in the late 1970's of becoming the more fashionable of the two.

Mary (f)   Gaelic **Mairi, Moire** or **Muire.** After centuries of intensive usage throughout the English-speaking world (and in its various forms, throughout the Christian world), this name is slowly but definitely going out of fashion everywhere. In Scotland the name usually ran a close second to **Margaret,** but in 1958 **Elizabeth** pushed it into third place. A count made in 1975 shows that it has dropped away very considerably since then, as it has in the rest of Britain, the U.S.A., Canada and Australia.

The original meaning of the name is impossible to

decipher; all that can be said for certain is that Mary represents the Greek form of **Miriam.** The reasons for the name's immense popularity, in a Christian context, are obvious. The reasons for its decline are not necessarily connected with a turning away from Christianity; it is just a general fact that since the 1940's parents everywhere have been naming children less conservatively, using a much wider range of names than ever before and breaking away from names borne by relations. Mary is still with us, and will probably be increasingly used as a middle name. Those bearing the name are often known by a pet form such as **May, Minnie, Molly** or **Mamie.**

Matilda (f) Also **Mathilda.** An Old German name, composed of elements meaning 'might' and 'battle.' It was introduced to Britain in the eleventh century as the name of the wife of William the Conqueror. Its use in Scotland occurred mainly in the nineteenth century, when its pet form **Maud** was also to be found. Other pet forms include **Matty, Tilly** and **Tilda.**

Matthew (m) Hebrew, 'Jehovah's gift.' This name has been at the height of fashion in England and Wales in the late 1970's, whereas in Scotland it appears to be slowly disappearing. The name is 'new' in the South; Scottish parents have long been familiar with it. Matthew was 26th most frequently used name in Scotland in 1858, 38th in 1935 and 62nd in 1958. **Mat** is the usual pet form. The surname *Mathieson,* 'son of Matthew,' is used on occasion as a Christian name in Scotland. The *Mathesons* in the Highlands, however, are known collectively in Gaelic as *Mathanach,* from a name which originally meant 'son of the bear.'

Maureen (f) An Irish pet form of **Mary,** seen as **Mairin** in Ireland. **Moreen** is occasionally used as an alternative spelling. The name has been very popular in

Scotland this century, reaching 25th position by 1935 and 16th place by 1958. English and Welsh parents also took to the name around 1950. It has suffered the usual fate of names that become fashionable, for it has been little used in Scotland in the late 1970's.

Maurice (m) Latin, 'a Moor.' Usage of this name in Scotland probably reflects Irish ancestry. Maurice has long been used in Ireland as a substitute for **Muirgheas,** 'sea choice.' In the Highlands it also served, e.g., amongst the *Macraes,* as a substitute for **Muireach**—see **Murdo.** In Scotland the spelling **Morris** occurs, but this may derive from the surname (which itself derives from Maurice).

Maxwell (m) A Scottish placename (possibly 'the pool belonging to **Maccus**') turned surname. The *Maxwells* have been established in Scotland since the thirteenth century, and the name frequently occurs in the history of Border warfare. Maxwell is quite often used as a Christian name in Scotland, and is usually abbreviated to **Max.**

May (f) This is usually explained as a pet form of **Mary, Margaret,** etc, though in Scott's *Redgauntlet* (1824) a girl called Dorcas is addressed as 'my fair May,' May being used in its obsolete sense of 'maiden.' It was later associated with the name of the month, and may have influenced the use of **April, Avril** and **June.** May was most popular in Scotland at the turn of the century.

Melanie (f) Greek, 'black.' Recently Scottish parents have been using this name far more than ever before. It is also currently popular in other English-speaking countries. This may have something to do with the use of the name in Margaret Mitchell's great success, *Gone With The Wind* (1936), a novel which also became an immensely successful film, first shown in 1939. Melanie Hamilton in *Gone With The Wind* marries **Ashley** Wilkes, and Ashley has also been used with more intensity recently. A **Scarlett** was named in Scotland in 1958, as was a **Careen,** which was the name of one of Scarlett O'Hara's sisters. See also **Bonnie.**

Melville (m)   A Norman placename which was brought to Scotland as a surname. It is occasionally used as a Christian name. **Melvin** is another form of it, found both in early documents and in local Scottish pronunciation. Melvin also occurs as a Christian name, sometimes spelt as **Melvyn.**

Michael (m)   Gaelic **Mìcheil.** Hebrew, 'who is like God?' The name was in early use by the Scotts, e.g., Sir Michael Scot, son of Sir Michael Scot of Balwearie, was a famous thirteenth-century scholar known as 'The Wizard.' The name did not appear in the Scottish Registrar General's Report for 1858. The count of 1935, however, showed it to be in 28th place, and by 1958 it had risen to 12th position. It continues to be extremely popular with Scottish parents, as it is with their counterparts throughout the English-speaking world. The Gaelic form is **Mìcheil.** The feminine forms in use include the French **Michelle** (much used since the Beatles sang a song of that name), **Michele** (the usual spelling of the name in Scotland in the 1950's) and **Michella. Michaela** is also found.

Mildred (f)   An Old English name, composed of elements meaning 'mild' and 'strength.' It enjoyed a very minor spell of popularity around the turn of the century. For Helena Swan, writing in 1900 *(Girls' Christian Names)*, it was 'an extremely pretty old Anglo-Saxon name.' A character in Somerset Maugham's *Of Human Bondage* (1915), however, refers to it as 'an odious name . . . so pretentious.'

Moira (f)   A phonetic form of the Irish **Maire, 'Mary.'** Moira was in 33rd position in Scotland in 1935 and again in 1958. **Moyra** occurs as a variant.

Molly (f)   Gaelic **Maili.** A pet form of **Mary** occasionally used as an independent name in Scotland. 'I was christened Mary, but Papa likes Molly,' says a character in *Wives and Daughters* (1866), by Mrs Gaskell. 'That's right. Keep to the good old fashions,' is the reply. Black *(The Surnames of Scotland)* tells us that **Male** (=**Malie**) 'was a common forename for women in Edinburgh in the sixteenth century.'

Monica (f)   A name of unknown origin which is used especially by Roman Catholic parents in honour of St Monica. In 1958 only 23 girls born in Scotland received the name.

Morag (f)   A Gaelic diminutive of *mor*, 'great.' **Sarah** or **Marion** are the usual English substitutes. Morag was 58th most frequently used name in Scotland in 1935, 56th in 1958. It is still in quiet use.

Morna (f)   Gaelic *muirne,* 'beloved.' This name is quietly but regularly used in Scotland. In Ireland **Muirna** has been noted in recent times.

Morven (f)   Also **Morvern, Morvyn.** Scottish use of Morven seems to have increased in the late 1970's. Morven is the name of mountains in Aberdeenshire and Caithness; Morvern is the name of a district in North Argyll. In Macpherson's Ossianic poems (1765) Morven is loosely used to represent the whole of North-West Scotland. Fingal is called both 'King of Selma' and 'King of Morven,' **Selma** (which is also used as a Christian name) being the capital of Morven. The mountain name Morven is Gaelic *mór bheinn,* 'big ben,' i.e., 'big mountain peak.' Morvern is Gaelic *mór bhearna,* referring to the big pass or 'cleft' which runs through the district. Some reference books have confused Morven and Morvern with the name of a Cornish saint, **Morwenna,** a name still occasionally used in Cornwall. The original meaning of Morwenna is obscure, but it is no doubt related to other names such as **Morvoren,** 'mermaid,' where *Mor-* is 'sea'.

Muir (m)   A surname which derives from residence near a 'moor.' It is in occasional use as a Scottish Christian name.

Mungo (m)   See **Kentigern.** In J. I. M. Stuart's novel *Mungo's Dream* the hero is named, we are told, 'because there's a Mungo Lockhart in a Scottish poem my father's said to have been rather proud of.' The poem is William Dunbar's *Lament*. Mungo 'amiable,' was the nickname of St Kentigern, patron saint of Glasgow, and the name is still used especially in that area. The noted Scottish explorer Mungo Park (1771-1806) has also helped to make the name well known.

Munro (m)   Gaelic **Mac An Rothaich.** The origin of this clan name and surname is much disputed. It has been connected with the River Roe in Derry, the *Munros* being thought by some to be of Irish stock. Others rather doubtfully refer the name to *Ross*, as the family were formerly vassals of the earls of Ross. Munro, which also takes the form **Monro,** is in occasional use as a Scottish Christian name.

Murdo (m)   The usual spelling in Scotland of **Murdoch** when used as a Christian name. It derives from either of two Gaelic names, **Muireach** or **Murchadh** ('mariner' and 'sea warrior'). Murdo was obviously unfamiliar to the English Registrar who recorded the birth, in 1878, of **Murder** John Smith, son of Private Murder Smith of the Scots Guards. **Murdina** has been used as a feminine form of Murdo.

Muriel (f) Sir John Campbell of Inverliver carried off
and married Muriel, heiress of the Thane of Calder, in
1510. The affair cost the lives of six of Inverliver's seven
sons, who were killed by Muriel's relations, but it led to
the founding of the *Campbells* of Calder (or Cawdor).
As for the name's meaning Woulfe, in his *Irish Names For
Children*, has no doubt that it is the anglicised form of
Muirgheal, 'sea bright,' or 'fair one of the sea.' Mrs
Craik focused attention on the name in her novel, *John
Halifax, Gentleman* (1856), using it to name the hero's eldest
child who is subsequently discovered to be blind. Perhaps for this reason, and because Mrs Craik herself
describes the name in the book as 'rather peculiar,' it
did not become very popular. It was used rather more in
the 1920's, but it has since faded away. Another literary
reference is to be found in Jane Duncan's novel *My Friend
Muriel* (1959): 'Muriel came floating towards me in the grey
cloud of the unattractiveness of her name.'

Murray (m) Gaelic **Moirreach.** A surname deriving
from the Scottish placename Moray. Both Murray and
Moray are used in Scotland as Christian names, *Murray*
being the more usual spelling. The name is also much used
by Canadian parents of Scottish origins.

Myles (m) *Myles* rather than **Miles** is the usual Scottish
spelling of this name. It was apparently introduced as an
English substitute for the Gaelic **Mael-Moire**, 'devotee of
the Virgin Mary.' The name has never been especially
popular, though it is used in Skye by the *MacInneses*.

Myra (f) This name is perhaps an English form of
Greek **Myrrha**, borne by the mother of *Adonis*. It seems
to have been used first in English by the writer, Fulke
Greville, in the seventeenth century. Since it was then the
fashion to invent new names for poetic purposes, Myra may
simply have been an anagram of **Mary.** Other possibilities

include a shortening, and respelling, of such names as **Mirabel, Miranda,** or a direct play on the word 'admire.' The name has been used more in Scotland this century than anywhere else in the English-speaking world. For Scottish parents it no doubt recalls by its sound names like **Moira** and **Muriel.**

N

Nancy (f) Originally an extension of **Nan,** or a variation of **Nanny,** both of which are pet forms of **Ann.** Nancy has long been in use as an independent name, though it has not been fashionable in Scotland in the last hundred years. In the U.S.A. and Canada, by contrast, the name was an immense success in the early 1950's.

Neil (m) This is the usual form in Scotland of a name that also appears as **Nigel.** The spellings **Neal, Neale, Neill, Niel** and **Niall** are also found. Niall is probably the 'correct' form of this Irish name, which means 'champion.' It is not clear whether it was translated into Latin as **Nigellus** because it was wrongly thought to mean 'black,' or whether Nigellus was used for euphony, then wrongly retranslated. At all events, Neil and Nigel were explained as deriving from Latin *niger*, 'black,' in many early reference works.

Neil has long been popular in Scotland. It was 23rd most frequently used name in 1858, 37th in 1935, 32nd in 1958. In 1975 Scottish parents were still using it a great deal. Nigel has never been as much of a success outside Scotland, though English and Welsh parents suddenly began to use it in large numbers from 1955-65. Scottish opinion of Nigel may be reflected by the comments of a character in Gordon McGill's novel *Arthur :* 'Your mother wanted to call you Nigel . . . a pansy name, like a duke. But I was too quick.'

The feminine forms **Neilena** and **Neilina** were both used in Scotland in 1958.

Nessie (f)   A Scottish diminutive of **Agnes,** and internationally famous as the playful name of the Loch Ness Monster.

Neville (m)   The surname *Neville* comes from Normandy, where Neuville 'new town' is a common placename. As a Christian name Neville (the usual Scottish spelling) or **Nevil** has been in use since the seventeenth century.

Nicholas (m)   Gaelic **Neacal, Macneacail.** A Greek name composed of elements meaning 'victory' and 'people.' **Nicol** was the early spelling leading its use in Scotland to surnames such as *MacNicol(l)*. The intrusive *h* appeared in the Middle Ages and has remained unnecessarily ever since. During the last hundred years neither form of the name has appealed greatly to Scottish parents, though Nicholas has been extremely well used in England and Wales since 1955. The pet form **Colin** is now used as an independent name. Another diminutive in former times was **Colley.** A correspondent, Mr Willie McRobert, of Ayr, reports that Nicholas was used as a girls' name in the Galloway region until fairly recently.

Nicola (f)   This is the Italian form of **Nicholas,** the Italian feminine form being **Nicoletta.** Nicola is now well established as a girls' name in Britain; elsewhere in the English-speaking world the French feminine form **Nicole** is preferred. Nicola was the name given to only 25 girls born in Scotland in 1958. Since then it has taken Scotland by storm. It has also been immensely successful in England and Wales since 1955. Other feminine forms of Nicholas used in Scotland include **Nichole** and **Nicolette,** the latter leading to **Colette** or **Collette.**

Ninian (m) 'Ninian is now almost entirely Scottish' says
The Oxford Dictionary of English Christian Names (1977).
Be that as it may, not a single boy born in Scotland in
1958 received the name, nor did it make an appearance
in a count of Scottish names made in 1975.

Black *(Surnames of Scotland)* tells us that Ninian became
Ringan in vernacular Scots, and as such 'was a common
forename in the 16th century and later.' This form of the
name has also fallen out of use. St Ninian, whose name
appeared in early sources as **Nynia, Ninnidh** as well as
Ninian, was a missionary who exercised considerable
influence amongst the Celts in the fifth century.

Nora, Norah (f) These short forms of **Eleanor(a)** were
being used to some extent in Scotland from 1900-35.
The name was frequently extended to **Noreen.** All three
forms are still in occasional use.

Norma (f) A name that was almost unknown in the
English-speaking world until the American actress Norma
Shearer began to appear on cinema screens in the 1920's.
Norma then had a fashionable run in the U.S.A. and
Canada, and was used to some extent in England and Wales.
Scottish parents took to the name immediately as a suitable
feminine form of **Norman.** By their extensive use of the
name they have to a large extent made it their own. It
reached 47th position in Scotland in 1935, but it then
dropped to 82nd place in 1958.

The name was known in musical circles because of
Bellini's opera *Norma,* based on a poem by Saumet. This
was first performed in 1831, but it is absurd to say, as do a
number of reference works, that Norma became a popular
name in the nineteenth century as a result. Such works often
add that Sir Walter Scott had a character called Norma in
The Pirate (1821), whereas the name he used there was
Norna, the name of one of the Fates in Scandinavian
mythology.

Norman(m) 'North man.' The name was formerly much
used in Scotland: it was 31st most frequently used name
in 1858; 29th in 1935; 50th in 1958. A 1975 count, however,
shows that it has fallen out of use. Black *(Surnames of Scotland)* tells us that the name was used as a substitute for the
Norse **Tormod,** or **Thormond,** names meaning 'Thor
minded' and 'Thor protected,' both of which, says Black,
were 'favourite names with the Macleods.' Norman was
much used in the U.S.A. from 1900, and it became fashionable in England and Wales between 1925 and 1935. It is now
rarely used anywhere. The usual feminine form is **Norma,**
but two girls born in Scotland in 1958 were named
Noramana.

O

Olive (f) The name of the olive tree has been used for
centuries as a personal name. It became fashionable in
Britain when botanical names were popular towards the end
of the nineteenth century. In Scotland the name was
reasonably well used until 1925. It was still in 83rd position
in 1935, but subsequently it dropped out of use. The
Italian form **Olivia** is sometimes used. Mrs Craik, in her
novel *Olive* (1850) went to some lengths to explain why her
central character bore such a 'strange, heathen name,' as the
servant describes it. Olive's mother is supposed to have had a
dream or vision in which an angel-child extended an olive
branch to her in moments of peril. Olive, of course, does
have this symbolic association with 'peace,' so that it could
be considered as a synonym of **Irene.**

Osla (f) In Shetland this name represents a survival of
Old Norse **Aslaug,** later **Aslög,** 'god consecrated.' Girls
bearing this name, according to A. T. Cluness in his book,
The Shetland Isles, had to be baptised by the more familiar,
acceptable name, **Ursula,** Latin 'little bear.'

Owen (m)   This Welsh name, said to be a form of the Latin
Eugenius, 'well born,' has had some recent success in
Scotland. See also **Ewan.**

P

Pamela (f)   Pamela was first used by Sir Philip Sidney
in his *Arcadia* (1590). Already familiar at that time was
the name **Pamphilus,** 'beloved of all,' which occurred in a
popular twelfth-century Latin poem. It was well enough
known to lead eventually to the word *pamphlet.* There had
earlier been several martyrs named Pamphilus, and modern
French ecclesiastical authorities regard Pamela as a feminine
version of that name. Samuel Richardson named his servant-
girl heroine Pamela in his novel of that name (1740), thus
making it a working-class name for centuries. This stigma
disappeared by the 1950's, when the name became generally,
but quietly, popular throughout Britain. It remains in steady
use in Scotland.

Parlan (m)   Gaelic *MacPharlain,* 'son of Parlan,' is the
origin of surnames such as *Macfarlane, Macfarland,* etc.
Parlan is still in occasional use as a Christian name in
Scotland. It represents the Irish **Parthalan,** a name
which has been explained as 'waves of the sea.' A man
bearing this name figures prominently in Irish legend, and
also in the family legends of the earls of Lennox. When
'English' names became obligatory in former times,
Bartholomew was seized upon as a substitute of Parlan.
As usual there was no etymological connection between the
two names. Bartholomew is Hebrew, meaning 'son of the
twin.' The name was formerly much used because of the
popularity of St Bartholomew. It gave rise to numerous
surnames, including *Bart, Bartle, Bartlet, Bates, Bateson,
Bateman, Batson,* etc. Bartholomew is now rare as a Scottish

Christian name, as is **Bartle,** a form once used in the Shetlands.

Patricia (f) The feminine form of **Patrick.** The French **Patrice** is also used occasionally in Scotland. Patricia was ranked 17th in Scotland in 1935, 13th in 1958. It has since fallen out of favour, not only in Scotland but in all other English-speaking countries. Of its pet forms, **Trish** and **Tricia** are currently far more in vogue than **Pat.** Some Scottish parents in the late 1970's have used Tricia as an independent name.

Patrick (m) Latin *patricius,* 'patrician,' originally one who was a 'father' or senator of Rome. The name could therefore be translated as 'Roman nobleman.' Patrick has long been associated with Ireland, but it was established very early in Scotland. Black *(Surnames of Scotland)* cites various Gaelic forms: **Padruig, Paruig, Para** and **Padair/Patair.** The last of these led to the belief in Scotland that **Peter** was simply a pet form of Patrick, or as Black picturesquely puts it, Patrick was thought to be the Sunday name, Peter the everyday one. In recent times Patrick was 23rd most frequently used name in Scotland in 1935, 35th in 1958. In the late 1970's it seems to have dropped out of fashion. **Pat** and **Paddy** are the usual diminutives, but they are rarely used as independent names. Many surnames derive from Patrick, including *Paterson, Patison, Pattison. Petrie* as a surname can refer to an ancestor who was either Patrick or Peter.

Paul (m) Latin *paulus,* 'small.' This is very much a name of the 1970's in the English-speaking world, though it has now begun to go out of fashion in the U.S.A. and Canada. Paul was 27th most frequently used name in Scotland in 1958, and it has become more popular since.

Its use in Scotland in the Middle Ages led to such surnames as *Polson* (from Gaelic **Pòl**), *Macphail, Paulin* and *Paulson.*

Pauline (f)   This is the normal feminine form of **Paul,** though **Paula** and **Paulette** are also used by Scottish parents. Pauline also occurs occasionally as **Pauleen** or **Paulene.** Pauline was very fashionable in England and Wales around 1950. It seems to have reached Scotland rather later. In 1958 it was 55th most frequently used name, and a 1975 count shows it to be still in favour. In other English-speaking countries Paula (originally a German feminine form much used in Germany in the nineteenth century) is replacing Pauline.

Pearl (f)   This name was given to 32 girls born in Scotland in 1958. In some cases there may have been a deliberate link with the name **Margaret,** which also means 'pearl.' Pearl is well known in American literature because of Nathaniel Hawthorne's novel *The Scarlet Letter* (1850). In this the heroine names her daughter Pearl 'as being of great price—purchased with all she had—her mother's only treasure.'

Peter (m)   Greek, 'stone.' Gaelic **Peadair.** This name was popular in all English-speaking countries in the period 1945-60. In Scotland it had long been a steady favourite, perhaps because of its supposed connection with **Patrick.** It was the 11th most frequently used name in Scotland in 1858, 12th in 1935, 14th in 1958. It has continued to be well used in Scotland in the late 1970's, but its very popularity is now beginning to cause a reaction against it. The modern popularity of the name outside Scotland was no doubt due to the Scottish playwright, J. M. Barrie. His *Peter Pan,* first staged in 1904, became an instant success.

Feminine forms of Peter include **Peta, Petra, Peterina** and **Petrina**. See also **Patrick**.

Philip (m)   Greek, 'lover of horses'. A name which has been quietly popular in Scotland this century. In former times in Fife, local pronunciation of the name led to the surname *Philp*. Philip was well used in England and Wales in the 1960's but it has subsequently fallen away. Feminine forms of the name used in Scotland include **Philippa (Pippa)** and **Philippe**.

Philomena (f)   Greek, 'I am loved.' The name of several saints, and the name of 23 girls born in Scotland in 1958.

Phyllis (f)   Greek, 'leafy.' This was the name of a Thracian princess who died of love and was metamorphosed into an almond tree. Various other legends are associated with the name. It was taken up by English poets in former times, often as **Phillida** or **Phillis,** and Robert Burns has a song called *Phillis the Fair*. The name was most used in Scotland around 1925.

Preston (m)   This former Scottish placename, now Craigmillar, became a surname which is occasionally used as a Christian name.

Q

Quintin (m)   Latin 'fifth.' The *i*-spelling seems to be usual in Scotland, but **Quentin,** as in Scott's *Quentin Durward* (1823), is also found. Saint Quentin of Amiens became patron saint of Kirkmahoe in Dumfriesshire. The name was most used in Scotland, especially in Galloway, before the seventeenth century.

R

Rachel (f)   Occasionally spelt **Rachael.** Hebrew, 'ewe.'
The name was no doubt used originally for its symbolic
meaning of 'gentleness.' Like many Old Testament names,
this was most used in Scotland in the nineteenth century
and earlier, often as a substitute for Gaelic **Raoghnaild,**
itself from Norse **Ragnhildr,** modern Swedish **Ragnhild,**
'battle counsel.' In England and Wales the name has
recently become fashionable. Scott has a character called
Rachel Waverley in *Waverley* (1814) and a Rachael in
Peveril of the Peak (1823).

Ralph (m)   An Old Norse or Old English name composed of elements meaning 'counsel' and wolf.' It was
formerly pronounced *Rafe*, as the Gilbertian verse indicates:
> In time each little waif
> Forsook his foster-mother,
> The well-born babe was Ralph—
> Your captain was the other.
> *(H.M.S. Pinafore)*

Ralph has been quietly used in Scotland this century.

Ramsay (m)   Also **Ramsey.** A placename which became
a surname, now occasionally used as a Christian name. The
original meaning of the name is explained by Ekwall as
'wild garlic island.' The *Ramsays* have been established in
Scotland since the twelfth century.

Raymond (m)   An Old German name composed of
elements meaning 'advice' and 'defence.' It became popular
in England and Wales from 1925-50, reaching Scotland
rather later. In 1958 Raymond was still the 39th most
frequently used name in Scotland, but it seems to have
faded away since then. The diminutive **Ray** is sometimes
used as an independent name, more frequently for girls
than boys and often in the form **Rae.** The girls' name
presumably derives from **Rachel.**

Rebecca (f) Also **Rebekah.** A Biblical name from a
Hebrew word of doubtful etymology. Scott's beautiful
Jewess in *Ivanhoe* (1819) is Rebecca; he also uses the
name for characters in *Guy Mannering* (1815) and *The
Antiquary* (1816). Rebecca (Becky) Sharp in Thackeray's
Vanity Fair (1847-8) is also one of the most famous
characters in English literature. The name was most used
in Scotland in the nineteenth century. Its recent return
to favour in England and Wales does not as yet seem to
have impressed Scottish parents.

Rhoda (f) Greek, 'rose.' A Biblical name that has occasionally been used in Scotland. It is said to be still very
popular in Palestine, in the Arabic form **Wardeh**.

Rhona (f) Apparently the same name, in a slightly
different guise, as **Rona,** both of which came into use as
Christian names at the beginning of the century. By 1950
both forms were being used to some extent in England
and Wales, but they are basically Scottish names. The
Scottish placename Rona appears to be the source. This
probably derives from Norse *hraun-ey*, 'rough isle.'

Rhonda (f) The use of this Welsh placename as a
Christian name in English-speaking countries seems to be
due to the actress Rhonda Fleming, who was christened
Marilyn (Louis). For the adoption of a placename as a
stage name, compare **Gary,** but Rhonda has not had the
same immense success.

Richard (m) An Old German name composed of elements meaning 'king' and 'firm.' Early use of the name in
Scotland is attested by surnames such as *Dick, Dickie,
Dickinson, Dickson, Dikin, Ritchie* and *Richieson*. **Ritchie**
is itself occasionally used as a Scottish Christian name.
Richard has been in consistent use in Scotland, as elsewhere in the English-speaking world, for centuries. The

name was in 28th position in Scotland in 1858, 30th in 1935, 31st in 1958. It has been intensively used in the late 1970's. Jane Austen wrote playfully in *Northanger Abbey* (1818) of 'a very respectable man, though his name was Richard.' Feminine forms such as **Ricarda** and **Richenda** occur very occasionally in Scotland.

Robert (m)   Gaelic **Raibeart.** An Old English name, originally meaning 'fame bright.' In Scotland the name was in 5th position in 1858, 4th in 1935, 5th in 1958. It continues to be one of Scotland's favourite names, as its many historical associations justify (it was, of course, the name of Scotland's national hero, Robert Bruce). The name is also immensely popular in every other English-speaking country. Robert Louis Stevenson in *The Weir of Hermiston* (1894) gives the 'proper Border diminutive' as **Hob,** which is now obsolete, though like **Dob** it led to surnames such as *Hob, Hobson, Dobbie, Dobieson, Dobson.* **Rab, Rabbie, Rob** and **Robbie** are the best-known Scottish diminutives, though **Bob** and **Bobby** are also in use.

Roberta (f)   This is the usual feminine form of **Robert** in Scotland, though **Robina** (pet form **Beanie**), **Robertina, Robena** and **Robyn** are also in use. Feminine forms of Robert have never been particularly fashionable, but the names are used steadily.

Robin (m)   In Scotland this is a male diminutive of **Robert.** Elsewhere, especially in the U.S.A., Robin is now a girls' name and the connection with Robert is forgotten. It continues to be a fairly popular male name with young parents in Scotland, but the sexual confusion will in-evitably spread, causing the name to be thought of as feminine only. In that role it is likely to be spelt **Robyn.**

Roderick(m) Old Germanic, 'fame rule.' The name often occurs in the clan histories, e.g., the *MacNeils*. It was the normal English substitute for Gaelic **Ruairidh,** 'red,' because of vague similarities of pronunciation. Roderick was heavily used in Scotland during the nineteenth century, being 27th most frequently used name in 1858. By 1935 it was in 60th position, and in 1958 it was 63rd. An unofficial name count made in 1975 suggests that Roderick was at that time coming back into fashion.

Roger (m) Old English, 'fame-spear.' A quietly used name in Scotland this century, and never especially fashionable. In England and Wales it was much used around 1950, but it has since been left aside.

Roland (m) This is used as a substitute in the Shetlands for Norse **Rognvald,** or **Ragnvald** in modern Swedish, 'ruler of unfavourable gods.' Roland, or **Rowland** as it often appears, is Germanic, composed of elements meaning 'fame' and 'land'.

Roman (m) This name, occasionally used in Scotland as a Christian name, may derive from surnames such as *Romanes, Romanis* or *Romans.* These, in turn, owe their origin to the placename *Romanno* ('fort,' 'circle of the monk'), in Peebleshire.

Ronald (m) The most popular form in Scotland, especially this century, of the Old English name **Regenweald** or Norse **Rögnvaldr,** 'power-might.' Other forms, which were formerly much in use, include **Ranald** and **Reginald. Reynold** is yet another variant. Ronald was 37th most frequently used name in Scotland in 1858, 14th in 1935, 22nd in 1958, but it now seems to be liitle used. The name became popular in England and Wales around 1925, then reached the U.S.A. in force some twenty years later. In these countries too, however, it is

now out of fashion. The Gaelic form is **Raghnall. Rona**
is probably used in some cases as a feminine form of Ronald.

Rory (m)   Gaelic   **Ruairidh,**   or   **Ruaridh,**   'red.'
Roderick is also used as the English substitute for the
same Gaelic name, but Rory remains in consistent use in
Scotland.

Rosalind (f)   Old German, 'horse-serpent.' The serpent
was symbolic of wisdom, while the horse was worshipped
as a god in ancient times. Shakespeare was fond of this
name, using it in *As You Like It*. He also has a **Rosaline**
in *Romeo and Juliet* and *Love's Labour's Lost*. Rosalind
has been quietly but consistently used in Scotland.

Rose (f)   This name has long been identified with the
flower. It became popular in Scotland as elsewhere in the
English-speaking world when flower names were fashionable at the end of the nineteenth century. In ancient times
it was probably a shortened form of names like **Rosalind**
and **Rosamund,** where the first element is Old German
hros, 'horse.' A great many diminutive and foreign forms
of Rose have been used in Scotland, amongst which one
may include **Rosaleen, Rosalie, Rosalin, Rosalina,
Rosaline, Rosalyn, Rosalynn, Roseanna, Rosanne,
Rosealine, Roseann, Roseanna, Roseanne, Rosel,
Roselane, Roseleen, Roselinda, Roseline, Roselle,
Rosellen, Roselyn, Roselynn, Rosetta, Rosette, Rosey,
Rosina, Rosita, Roslyn, Roslynn, Rosslyn.** The
Latinised **Rosa** also occurs. Helena Swan *(Girls' Christian
Names)* mentions **Rosaura,** which she says means 'breath
of a rose,' but this seems to derive from her poetic
inventiveness rather than actual usage of the name. In a
Scottish context it must not be forgotten that *Rose* is the
name of a small Nairnshire clan. This fact may at times
have influenced the name's usage.

Rosemary (f)   Also **Rosemarie.** This name, hardly used
in the English-speaking world until the 1920's, was most
used in the 1950's by Scottish parents. It was 47th most
frequently used name in Scotland in 1958. The flower is
a symbol of remembrance, a fact played upon by E. C.
Stedman (1833-1908) in a poem to his godchild which
begins:

> Rosemary! could we give you
> 'Remembrance' with your name,
> Ere long you'd tell me something
> Of Heaven, whence you came . . .

Ross (m)   Gaelic **Ros, Rosach.** A placename in Scotland
and a distinguished Scottish surname, established since the
twelfth century. The surname derives from one of the places
called Ross, originally meaning 'moor' or 'cape,' 'peninsula,'
or from French *rousse*, 'red.' Ross is currently being well
used a Christian name in Scotland, Canada and (especially)
Australia.

Rowena (f)   A name of uncertain origin, occasionally
used in Scotland. Rowena is the heroine of Scott's novel
Ivanhoe (1819).

Roy (m)   An anglicised form of Gaelic *ruadh*, 'red.' Roy
was most used in Scotland, as in England and Wales, *circa*
1925. Scott's *Rob Roy* (1817) may have had some bearing
on the name's earlier usage.

Russell (m)   The use of this surname (which ranked
48th in Scotland in 1976) as a Christian name in modern
times seems to have begun in the U.S.A. in the latter half
of the nineteenth century. It probably honoured General
David Russell, who fought at Gettysburg in 1863 and was
killed at Opequan Creek a year later. English commen-
tators on the name have always assumed that the aristocratic family name was being used, but there is no reason

why this should be so. Russell has been used as a Christian name in Scotland since 1920. It was at its most popular in the 1950's, when it was also taken up to some extent in England and Wales. The surname is a diminutive form of French *roux*, 'red.'

Ruth (f) From the Biblical *Book of Ruth*, but the origin of this Hebrew name is obscure. It has been reasonably well used in Scotland this century, though never an outstanding favourite. This may change, as the name has been very fashionable in the late 1970's in other English-speaking countries.

Ryan (m) This Irish surname has recently been extremely popular as a Christian name in the U.S.A. and Canada. Since 1970 it has also been used throughout Britain. A recent count of Scottish Christian names (1975) makes it clear that Scottish parents have accepted it whole-heartedly. It was possibly introduced by, and has certainly been much publicised by, the American actor Ryan O'Neal. He appeared in the highly successful *Love Story* (1972) and has starred in several films since then.

There is a long discussion about the origin of the name in Maclysaght's *Surnames of Ireland,* which concludes that no exact etymology can be given.

S

Samantha (f) A name launched by the film *High Society* (1956), in which Grace Kelly played the part of **Tracy Samantha** Lord.

The origin of the name is in fact shrouded in mystery. It is listed in *Black Names In America* amongst female slave names in use before 1864. It may therefore be a feminine and fanciful version of **Samuel,** especially since the same list of names contains **Samella,** a shortened form of **Samuella.**

The television series *Bewitched* further publicised the name and associated it with witchcraft. This caused it to become a popular name for a cat in the U.S.A. Scottish parents, like those in England and Wales, consider the name to be perfectly suitable for their daughters, and they have been using it intensively in recent years.

Samuel(m) A Hebrew name of obscure meaning, though it contains the word 'God.' Samuel was rather popular in Scotland until recent times. In England and Wales it has been little used this century, though it has aroused interest in both countries in the late 1970's. In Scotland the name was 20th most frequently used in 1858, 31st in 1935 and 57th in 1958. In spite of the fall-off in the 1950's, Scottish parents were undoubtedly using the name with more intensity at that time than parents elsewhere in the English-speaking world. One reason for the name's relative popularity in Scotland may be its use as a substitute for Gaelic **Somhairle, Somerled,** or **Sorley** (a borrowing from a Norse name meaning 'summer sailor,' 'Viking').

Sandra (f) This is a short form of **Alexandra.** It was used as a separate name in several countries, for example, Italy, Yugoslavia, Rumania, Finland, before being used as such (in the early 1930's) in English-speaking countries. The reason for its sudden appearance in Britain and elsewhere is not clear. It had been mentioned, and indeed made much of, in George Meredith's novel *Emilia in England* (subsequently renamed *Sandra Belloni*), published in 1864. In the book Sandra is the daughter of an exiled Italian and an Englishwoman. However, this novel can hardly have been responsible, as Eric Partridge *(Name This Child)* suggests, for popularising the name.

Sandra was listed in *What Shall We Name the Baby?*

published in the U.S.A. in 1935, but this is no indication that the name was in general use there. The book contains a great many exotic names which have never been very common in English-speaking countries (e.g. **Zandra,** another form of Sandra; **Lexine,** a derivative of Alexandra; **Alyssa,** 'probably a form of **Alice**'). At the time of publication Sandra could have been as strange as these.

The Registrar General's Report on Scottish Christian names used in 1935 makes no mention of Sandra. The Report for 1958 shows it to be Scotland's 17th most frequently used name. It was by then as popular, if not more so, in the U.S.A., England and Wales. The latest counts in all these countries seem to indicate that parents have now abandoned the name as thoroughly as they adopted it a short while ago.

Sarah (f)   Hebrew, 'princess.' This name has been highly fashionable in the late 1970's in every English-speaking country, including Scotland. The name was ranked 15th in Scotland in 1858, 12th in 1935, then it fell to 54th place in 1958. Normally this would have been a clear sign that the name was going to drop out of use for a considerable time, but it has recovered strongly. **Sally,** originally a pet form of Sarah, but used since the eighteenth century as an independent name, has also been popular in recent times. **Sadie,** another diminutive, has also been used as a name in its own right, though never to any great extent. The spelling **Sara** is occasionally used by Scottish parents, and this can lead to a slight difference in pronunciation of the name, the first syllable rhyming with *far* rather than *stare*. Sarah is often used as a substitute for Gaelic **Mór(ag).**

Scott (m)   The surname *Scott* could hardly be more Scottish from both an etymological and historical point of view. However all the evidence indicates that its use as a Christian name began in the U.S.A. It was certainly far more popular there by 1950 than in Scotland itself, though Scottish parents later gave the name the warmest of welcomes. Scott is in fact likely to become one of Scotland's top names in the 1980's. The name is also rapidly gaining ground in England and Wales.

American usage was undoubtedly influenced by the writer Scott Fitzgerald (1896-1940), who was well-known from 1920 onwards. He was born Francis Scott Key Fitzgerald, and was of Irish rather than Scottish descent.

The Christian name derives directly from the surname (the 12th most frequent in Scotland in 1976), which means 'a Scot.' Some parents prefer to spell the name without the extra *t*, emphasising that it means what it says. The parents of one boy born in Scotland in 1958 went still further, interpreting Scot(t) as a pet form and bestowing on their son the Christian name **Scotland.**

Sean (m) An Irish form of **John** made famous in recent times by the Scottish actor Sean Connery in the role of James Bond. The name is sometimes spelt phonetically as **Shaun.** The latter form has become a popular replacement for John in Scotland in the late 1970's. **Shauna** and **Shaune** are occasionally used to name Scottish girls.

Senga (f) A back-spelling of **Agnes.** The name is only found in Scotland. Back-spellings of various names are used from time to time, e.g. **Azile, Cire** (pronounced *Kirry*), **Adnil,** but Senga has become relatively widespread in its usage where most names of the type remain oddities. The name presumably has a literary source, but it has not yet come to light. In 1958, 36 girls born in Scotland received this name.

Sharon (f) A placename, from Western Palestine, of an area renowned for its fertility. As the flower name, 'rose of Sharon,' it is mentioned in the Biblical *Song of Solomon*, or *Song of Songs*. Solomon has taken a Shulamite maiden to his court and pleads for her love, but she remains faithful to her shepherd lover. Her faithfulness is eventually rewarded when she is reunited with him. The Shulamite maiden is referred to in the song as the 'rose of Sharon,' and it is no doubt this reference which led to the adoption of Sharon as a girls' name. As it happens, the original flower called the rose of Sharon was probably not a rose at all, but a narcissus or crocus, but the flower name was established by this usage as symbolic of feminine beauty. Sir Walter Scott uses it that way in *Ivanhoe* (1819): 'I am not an outlaw, then, fair Rose of Sharon.'

Use of Sharon as a Christian name began in the seventeenth century, according to Miss E. G. Withycombe (*Oxford Dictionary of Christian names*), who also says that it could be used as a male name at that time. In modern times the name has been exclusively female and it has enjoyed a spell of great popularity, first in the U.S.A. and Canada, later in Britain. Sharon was at its peak in England and Wales in 1970 but it has subsequently fallen away rapidly. In Scotland the name has been one of the most frequently used girls' names in the late 1970's. It is also found as **Sharron, Sharyn** and **Sharonne.**

Sheena (f)   The usual spelling in Scotland of Gaelic **Sine,** '**Jean.**' It also occurs as **Sheana, Sheenah, Sheenagh, Shena, Sheona, Shiona, Shione.** Sheena was ranked 74th in Scotland in 1935 and it held the same position in 1958. In the 1970's the spelling *Sheona* appears to have gained ground. **Seonaid,** which is also used, is a Gaelic form of **Janet.**

Sheila (f)   Also   **Sheelagh,   Sheelah,   Sheilagh, Shelagh, Shiela.** These are phonetic forms of the Scottish and Irish **Sile,** itself a form of **Celia.** Sheila was popular in England and Wales from 1920-55. In Scotland it reached 15th position in 1935, then fell to 32nd place in 1958. It has continued to be used by Scottish parents in the late 1970's, but appears to be rapidly going out of fashion.

Shirley (f) This name was used sporadically in Britain after the publication of Charlotte Bronte's novel, *Shirley*, in 1849. It was not until 1934, however, when Shirley Temple became internationally famous as a child film-star, that the name became a favourite in all English-speaking countries. It had begun to be popular in the U.S.A. in the 1920's for reasons that are not clear, but it was possibly transferred from a surname. Apart from being a surname, Shirley is also a placename in England.

Scottish parents remained faithful to the name once they had decided to adopt it in the 1930's. In 1935 they made it the 43rd most frequently used name in Scotland. It became far more popular before falling away slightly to 52nd place in 1958. A count made in 1975 shows that it is still being quietly used.

Sholto (m) This name is occasionally found in the clan histories. A derivation from a Gaelic word meaning 'sower' or 'propagator' has been suggested.

Shona (f) This is the usual Scottish phonetic spelling of Gaelic **Seonaid,** a feminine form of **John** which could be anglicised as **Jane, Jean** or **Joan.** Other spellings include **Shonag, Shonagh, Shonah, Shone.** In some cases, it merges with **Sheena,** e.g. **Sheona.** Shona is consistently used in Scotland, but the name has never been especially fashionable.

Shuard (m) According to A. T. Cluness in his book, *The Shetland Isles,* this was, until recent times, a survival in the Shetlands of Norwegian **Sigurd. George** was also used as a substitute for this name. Sigurd, 'victory protector,' is a Scandinavian name which also appears as **Sigvard, Sigvart, Siver, Sivert, Sjur, Syver, Syvert, Siegward.**

Simon (m) A form of the Hebrew **Shimeon,** 'God has heard.' **Simeon** is an alternative form. Historically it is associated with the *Frasers*. The Chief of Clan Fraser of Lovat is styled *MacShimi*, 'son of Simon.' Simon was formerly a much-used name in Scotland, together with its pet forms **Sim, Sime, Sym, Syme, Simmie.** These gave rise to many surnames, such as *Simpkins, Simpson* and *Simson*. In more recent times Simon has been immensely popular in England and Wales, but it has been quietly used in Scotland in the late 1970's. Some of the surnames deriving from the name, such as *Simpson*, are occasionally used as Christian names in Scotland.

Sinclair (m)   A Norman placename which was transferred to Scotland as a surname as early as the twelfth century. An offshoot of the family held the earldom in Caithness until 1542. Sinclair is now occasionally used as a Christian name. It is a form of Saint Clare, a placename in Pont d'Eveque, Normandy. The Gaelic surname *Mac Na Ceaird* is also rendered as Sinclair, though *Tinkler* ('Tinker') would be more correct.

Sinnie (f)   A traditional name in the Shetlands, probably representing Scandinavian **Signe,** earlier **Signild, Siganhilt.** The forms **Signil** and **Signilla** also occur. The original meaning of the name was 'new victory.'

Sonia (f)   Also **Sonja, Sonjia, Sonya.** These spellings represent a Russian pet form of **Sofia (Sophia).** All forms are consistently but quietly used in Scotland.

Sophia (f)   Also **Sophie.** Greek, 'wisdom.' Both forms of the name were used in Scotland, and in the rest of Britain, during the nineteenth century, but they occur only rarely today. See also **Beathag.**

Stanley (m)   This common English placename, meaning a 'stony meadow,' became a surname, then a Christian name. The explorer Stanley found Dr Livingstone in 1871, which brought the name very much into the news. Stanley Baldwin became prime minister much later, but he received his name in 1867. By 1900 Stanley was a common Christian name throughout Britain, and it remained in fashion for a generation. In Scotland the name was in 43rd position in 1935, but it then faded away.

Stella (f)   Latin, 'star.' **Estelle**, the French form of the name, is also occasionally used. Roman Catholics might well have the Virgin Mary in mind when giving this name to their daughters, for one of her titles is *Stella maris,* 'star of the sea.' The name also has many literary associations, especially in the writings of Sir Philip Sidney (1554-86) and Jonathan Swift (1667-1745). Stella is regularly used in Scotland, but it has never been one of the more fashionable names.

Stephanie (f)   The feminine form of **Stephen.** It has been little used in Scotland, but with the popularity in the late 1970's of **Stephen/Steven** it will be surprising if use of Stephanie does not increase.

Stephen, Steven (m)   In recent times the spelling *Steven* has overtaken *Stephen* in Scotland, as in all other English-speaking countries. The name was originally Greek and meant the 'crown' or 'garland' worn by a victor. Stephen was in 18th position in Scotland in 1958, with Steven in 36th place. In a 1975 count of names given to Scottish boys, Steven was used twice as often as Stephen. The combined name, Stephen/Steven, was certainly one of Scotland's top names in 1958, and it has remained so in the late 1970's. It has also enjoyed a run of enormous popularity in recent years in all English-speaking countries. The short form **Steve** is often given as an independent

name. Scott has a character in *Redgauntlet* (1824) called
Stephen Stephenson, or Steenson, who is addressed as
Steenie. *Steen* was in fact the early pronunciation of
Stephen in Fife and the Lothians, leading to such surnames
as *Steen* and *Stein, Staines* and *Steinson.*

Struan (m) A Clan *Donachie (Robertson)* name, the
chiefs formerly possessing the lands of Struan, or Strowan,
in Perthshire. It is doubtfully said to derive from 'little
stream.' Struan is occasionally used in Scotland as a
Christian name.

Stuart (m) Also **Stewart.** Gaelic **Stiùbhart.** This
famous surname originally meant 'steward,' i.e., 'chief of the
royal household.' The House of Stuart or Stewart ruled
in Scotland from 1371, and in England from 1603, until
1714. *Stuart,* which is now the preferred Scottish spelling
of the Christian name, is the French form used by Mary,
queen of Scots. Not surprisingly, Stuart and Stewart are
used more in Scotland than in any other English-speaking
country. Considered as one name, Stuart/Stewart was in
the Scottish top twenty in 1958. Both forms of the name
continue to be well used (occasionally for girls as well as
boys in the Galloway region).

Susan (f) Hebrew, from a word formerly meaning 'lily,'
and now used for 'rose.' **Susanna(h)** is the fuller form.
Other forms include **Susanne, Suzann, Suzanne.** Susan
was the name of names in the English-speaking world in
the 1950's, a top favourite in every country. Scottish
parents had long been using it. It was 26th most frequently
used name in Scotland in 1858, 36th in 1935, 7th in 1958. A
count of names used in Scotland in 1975 shows that it was
still being used in great numbers, though many parents
preferred the form Suzanne. The Gaelic form is **Siùsaidh.**
  The name owed its original popularity to the Apocryphal

story of Susanna and the Elders, an exciting tale of
detective work by Daniel which saved the life of the
beautiful Susanna. She had been falsely accused of adultery
by the Elders, who were furious when she refused their
advances. Daniel interrogated the Elders separately,
showing that their versions of what had happened did not
agree. They were put to death for telling lies, a fate which
Susanna herself would have suffered but for Daniel's inter-
vention. She was instead restored to her husband Joachim.

Sukey was once the diminutive of Susan, but this now
seems to be obsolete. **Sue** is occasionally given as an
independent name.

Sydney (m) The preferred spelling in Scotland of a name
also found as **Sidney.** The Christian name is a transferred
use of the surname, which in turn is a reduction of 'Saint
Denis.' The name was very popular in Britain from 1875-
1925, but it then faded away. In Scotland it was in 61st
position in 1935. The late nineteenth-century popularity
of the name may have owed something to Sydney Carton,
in Dickens's *Tale of Two Cities* (1859), who heroically
sacrifices himself, taking the place of Darney on the
guillotine. His famous last thought was: 'It is a far, far
better thing that I do, than I have ever done; it is a far, far
better rest that I go to than I have ever known.'

Sylvia (f) A feminine form of the Latin name **Silvanus,**
borne by the god of woods and forests (Latin *silva,* 'wood').
Silvanus has been used in Scotland on occasions, sometimes
spelt as **Sylvanus. Silas** is a variant of the name, and
Sylvester is connected etymologically.

Shakespeare asked the famous poetic question: 'Who is
Silvia ?' and many other pastoral poems of the seventeenth
century include the name. Burns wrote of *Damon and
Sylvia.* Sylvia was reasonably well used in Scotland from
1950-60, but it now seems to be out of fashion.

T

Terence (m)   Also **Terrence.** Terence (*c.* 195-159 B.C.),
the Roman comic poet, was born in Carthage but went to
Rome at an early age. He became the slave of Publius
Terentius Lucanus, a senator who eventually gave him his
freedom. As the black American slaves were later to do,
Terence adopted the name of his ex-master. The original
meaning of Terentius (Terence) is unknown.

Terence was popularly used in Ireland as a substitute for
a native name, **Toirdealbhach,** or **Turlough,** which
probably corresponds to modern Norwegian **Torlaug** or
Tallaug, meaning 'Thor wide,' or 'shaped like Thor.'
Terence became fashionable in England and Wales around
1950, when its use also increased in Scotland. Scottish
parents used it for the next ten years or so before leaving it
aside. The pet form **Terry** sometimes occurs as an independent name, but this is often feminine, a nickname from
Teresa.

Teresa, Theresa (f)   *Theresa* is the slightly more common
spelling of this name in Scotland, which in Greek possibly
meant 'inhabitant of Thera' (now Thira or Santorin). This
is an island in the Aegean Sea which has known many
volcanic eruptions. One of them, in the fifteenth century
B.C., may have given rise to the Atlantis legend. As the
name of a popular saint, Teresa has long been favoured by
Roman Catholic families. The name was in 45th place in
Scotland in 1935, when Teresa and Theresa were counted
together. In 1958 Theresa was ranked 75th, Teresa 100th.
Terese, Therese and **Theresia** are occasionally found.
The pet forms are **Terry, Tessa** and **Tracy,** all of which
are used as independent names.

Thomas (m)   Originally a nickname used to distinguish
one of three **Judahs** in the New Testament. Thomas
was a word in Aramaic meaning 'twin.' As the name of an

Apostle it has long been in use in all Christian countries. In Scotland the name was placed 8th in 1858, 7th in 1935, 6th in 1958, and it has remained extremely popular in the late 1970's. The feminine forms **Thomasina, Thomasena** and the Cornish **Tamsin** are also used occasionally by Scottish parents. The pet forms of the male name, **Tom** and **Tommy,** occur as independent names. The *Mactavishes* are descendants of a Thomas, or **Tammas** in its Lowland Scots form. In Gaelic the name is *MacThamhais*. The later Gaelic form is **Tomás.** *Chambers Twentieth Century Dictionary* records **Thomasa** and **Tomina** as feminine forms of Thomas, but examples are hard to find.

Thora (f)   A feminine form of the name of the god **Thor.** George Mackay Brown's novel set in the Orkneys, *The Sun's Net* (1976), seems to indicate that it is in use there.

Timothy (m)   Greek, 'honour God.' This was used in Scotland and in Ireland as a substitute for the native **Tadhg,** which means 'poet' or 'philosopher' (c.f. *MacCaig,* 'son of Tadhg'). **Thaddeus** was also used to anglicise this name, but Timothy is now common. Use of Timothy in Scotland may well have been influenced by its Irish usage. The name began to be used in significant numbers in Scotland, as well as in England and Wales, around 1960. It has been used in the late 1970's, but does not seem destined to become one of the more fashionable names.

Torquil (m)   A Torquil was founder of the *MacLeods* of Lewis, and the name is much used by that clan. It represents an adaptation into English of the Gaelic **Torcall/Torcaill,** itself a form of a Norse name which has various modern forms, e.g., **Torkel, Torkell, Torkild, Torkjell, Terkel.** The first part of the name is **Thor;** the second element is obscure. Torquil is little used in Scotland but somehow manages to have an aristocratic ring to it. There is a character who bears this name in Scott's *Fair Maid of Perth* (1828).

Tracy(f)   Also **Tracey.** Originally a pet form of **Teresa,** though **Terry** or **Terrie** is now more usual in that role. The modern use of Tracy (less often Tracey) owes much to the film *High Society* (1956) in which Grace Kelly played the part of Tracy Samantha Lord. **Samantha** and **Kelly** as girls' names also seem to date from that time. Tracy has been a huge success in England and Wales in recent years. It has been intensively used in Scotland in the late 1970's.

Trevor (m)   Predominantly a Welsh name, in usage and origin, but not uncommon in Scotland since 1950. Trefor Rendall Davies says, in his *Book of Welsh Names*, that Trevor anglicises **Trefor,** which is Welsh for either 'great homestead' or 'homestead by the sea.' It was originally a placename which became a surname before being transferred to use as a Christian name.

Tristram (m)   A name used by the *Gorthy* family of Perthshire for nearly 400 years. It occurs occasionally in modern Scotland. The name derives from Celtic *Drest* or *Drust*, 'tumult,' but it was associated in France with the word *triste*, 'sad,' and turned into **Tristan.** In the Arthurian legends Tristan (or Tristram) is said to have been so named because he was born in sorrow, his mother dying in childbirth. Tristram is also famous in literature because of the eighteenth-century novel by Laurence Sterne, *Tristram Shandy*.

Turval (m)   A survival in the Shetlands of Norse **Thorvald,** or **Torvald, Torald,** 'Thor ruler.'

U

Una (f)   An ancient and once common Irish name, phonetically spelt as **Oonagh** or **Oona. Uny** is another

Irish form, which perhaps explains why **Winny,** the pet
form of **Winifred,** was often used as a substitute for it.
Others took the name to be the same as **Unity,** one of
the Puritan abstract-quality names. **Agnes** was also thought
to translate the name, in the belief that Una derived from
Irish *uan*, 'lamb' and that Agnes also meant 'lamb' ('lamb'
in Latin is *agnus*). The original meaning of the Irish Una
is in fact unknown. It is not the same name as Spenser's Una
in the *Faerie Queene* (1590, 1596), where the Latin feminine
of *unus*, 'one' is clearly the intended meaning. Una continues to be used to some extent in Scotland. There is a
character bearing the name in Scott's *Waverley* (1814).

V

Valerie (f)   This derives from a Roman clan name,
probably based on Latin *valere*, 'to be strong.' First use of
the name in Britain was in the form **Valeria,** but the French
Valerie soon became more popular. Valerie became especially fashionable around 1950, and reached 46th position
in Scotland in 1958. It is now little used. The masculine
forms of the name, **Valerius** and **Valerio,** do not seem
to have been imported into Britain.

Vera (f)   Russian, 'faith.' The name came to Britain *circa*
1880 and had become extremely popular in England and
Wales by 1925. It is quietly used in Scotland, but it has
never been a particular favourite.

Veronica (f)   James Boswell gave specific details about the
introduction of this name to Scotland in a note to his *Journal
of a Tour to the Hebrides* (1773). 'The saint's name of
Veronica was introduced into our family through my great
grandmother Veronica, Countess of Kincardine, a Dutch

lady of the noble house of Sommelsdyck.' Boswell gave the name to one of his own daughters.

The ultimate origin of the name is much disputed. St Veronica is said to have been the woman of Jerusalem who wiped the face of Jesus with a cloth as he went to Calvary. A relic preserved in Rome is said to be the actual cloth. This is called the 'vernicle' in English, a word which derives from 'veronicle,' which in turn is usually explained as meaning 'true image,' for the features of Christ's face are said to have been miraculously impressed upon it. If this interpretation is correct, then the relic was named first, and the name was subsequently transferred to the saint.

Some scholars see Veronica as a Latin variant of the Greek **Berenice,** 'peace bringer.' Veronica is still used in Scotland, especially by Roman Catholic families.

Victor (m)   This name means what it says. It was borne by several saints and a pope, but it was in popular use in Britain only from 1885-1930. It was in 74th place in Scotland in 1935, but it is now very rarely used.

Victoria (f)   Latin, 'victory.' Victoria was the Roman goddess of victory. Queen Victoria inherited the name from her mother, who was German. During the queen's reign (1837-1901) the name was very rarely used in Britain, but it has become extremely fashionable in England and Wales, as well as Scotland, since 1970. In Scotland many of the pet forms are also used as names in their own right. These include **Vicki, Vickie, Vicky** and **Vikki.**

Vincent (m)   Latin, 'conquering.' A popular name with Roman Catholic parents because of St Vincent de Paul (*c.* 1580-1660), but never generally fashionable in Scotland.

Violet (f)   This flower was associated in France with Napoleon. The violet was the secret badge worn by his followers during his exile, and Napoleon was toasted as

'General Violet,' for he had said that he would return in the violet season. In Scotland Violet seems to have been used as a Christian name since the sixteenth century. Charlotte Yonge remarks in her *History of Christian Names* that 'the Scottish love of floral names took hold of it, and Violets have flourished there ever since.' Violet was indeed 46th most frequently used name in Scotland in 1935, but it is now rarely given.

Vivien, Vivienne (f)   Also **Vivian, Vivianne, Viviene, Vyvien.** Vivian has also been used as a male name in Scotland. It derives from Latin *vivianus*, 'lively.' The girls' name is associated with the Lady of the Lake: Vivien in Tennyson's version of the poem; Vivienne in French, but this 'wily wanton,' or 'personification of shameless harlotry,' as she has been called, seems hardly suitable as a namesake. The name has been quietly used in Scotland, though it enjoyed a minor spell of popularity in the 1940's. This was no doubt a compliment to the actress Vivien Leigh (1913-67). Miss Leigh was christened Vivian, but made a point of changing it to Vivien.

W

Wallace (m)   This Scottish surname, made famous by the patriot William Wallace (*c.* 1272-1305), is regularly but quietly used in Scotland as a Christian name. The name originally meant 'Welshman,' or as Black *(Surnames of Scotland)* explained it, 'Strathclyde Briton.' Wallace is also used as a Christian name in the U.S.A.

Walter (m)   Gaelic **Bhàtar.** An Old German name, composed of elements meaning 'rule' and 'folk.' The Scottish Royal Family of Stuart descended from a Walter, but the name is naturally associated with the *Scotts*. The

Border clan used the name for generation after generation, and Sir Walter Scott (1771-1832) made it world famous. Walter has been a popular name in Scotland. It was ranked 17th in 1858, 32nd in 1935; but by 1958 it had dropped to 68th place. For the moment Scottish parents are making little use of the name, though it seems hardly conceivable that it should cease to be a living name in Scotland.

Wanda (f)   Originally a German name, possibly connected with the tribal name **Vandal.** In spite of the comment in *The Oxford Dictionary of English Christian Names* that 'Wanda has lately been used a good deal in England,' (a statement which name counts in no way confirm), the name has been most used this century in Scotland.

Ward (m)   A surname used as a Christian name in the Orkneys. It means 'guardian.'

Wendy (f)   First used by J. M. Barrie in his *Peter Pan* (1904). Originally Wendy was a nickname for Barrie himself, after a little girl referred to him as 'friendy-wendy.' The name became very popular in England and Wales from 1945-65. It was fairly well used in Scotland during the same period, but now seems to be less popular with young parents.

William (m)   Old Germanic, 'will, volition' and 'helmet.' The name became immensely popular in Scotland in the Middle Ages from the time of William the Lion, (1143-1214), brother of King Malcolm IV, whom he succeeded in 1165. Sir William Wallace, the thirteenth-century hero whose exploits have been celebrated by Scottish writers and poets ever since, ensured that the name would always be well used. The name was ranked 3rd in Scotland in 1858, 3rd again in 1935, 3rd again in 1958. It is still a

very popular name with Scottish parents, though its use
did begin to decline somewhat after 1965.

Willie is sometimes given as an independent name in
Scotland, as is the surname **Wilson.** The early use of
William led to its becoming a surname in many forms,
ranging from *Wilkie, Wilkin, Wilkinson,* to *Williamson,
Willicock, Willis, Willison, Wilson, Willock* and *Willocks.*
The Gaelic form of the name is **Uilleam.**

Wilma (f)   The most popular modern form in Scotland
of **Williamina** or **Wilhelmina,** both of which are also
used in their full forms. The first of these sometimes
appears as **Williamena.** Wilhelmina is the more Germanic
form of the name, deriving from **William.** Williamina
was ranked 27th in Scotland in 1858, and was in 26th
place in 1935. It subsequently fell out of fashion, though
it is often retained as a middle name. Apart from Wilma,
other derivatives used as independent names include **Elma,
Mina, Minnie,** and **Minella.**

Winifred (f)   Welsh, *Gwenfrewi,* 'blessed reconciliation.'
A popular name in Britain generally from 1880-1925. It was
still in 53rd position in Scotland in 1935, but now it is
little used.

Y

Yvonne (f)   A French diminutive of **Yve. Yvette** is
another diminutive form, but this has never been as popular
in Scotland as Yvonne. Both are said to derive ultimately
from the 'yew.' Yvonne suddenly came into fashion in the
late 1940's, which seems to indicate that the Canadian
actress Yvonne de Carlo had some influence. Scottish
parents have continued to use the name consistently in the
late 1970's. Elsewhere it has fallen out of fashion since 1970.

SELECT BIBLIOGRAPHY

Ames, Winthrop, *What Shall We Name The Baby?* 1935, Hutchinson.

Belden, Albert D., *What Is Your Name?* 1936, The Epworth Press.

Bice, Christopher, *Names For The Cornish*, 1970, The Lodenek Press.

Brogger, Waldemar, *Gyldendals Navne Leksikon*, 1958, Gyldendal Norsk Forlag. (Norwegian)

Brookes, Rev. Reuben S., and Brookes, Blanche, *A Guide to Jewish Names*, publ. by the authors.

Browder, Sue, *The New Age Baby Name Book*, 1975, Warner Books.

Brown, Ivor, *A Charm of Names*, 1972, The Bodley Head.

Burgio, Alfonso, *Dizionario dei Nomi Propri di Persona*, 1970, Ceschina. (Italian)

Camden, William, *Remains Concerning Britain*, 7th ed. 1674, rep. 1870, rep. 1974 E P Publishing (contains a chapter which is the earliest treatise in English on Christian names: another chapter on surnames).

Chambers Twentieth Century Dictionary, ed. A. M. Macdonald, rep. 1974, W. & R. Chambers. (Appendix: 'Some English Personal Names')

Collins' Gem Dictionary of First Names, 1968, Collins.

Dauzat, Albert, *Dictionnaire des Noms de Famille et Prénoms de France*, 1951, Larousse.

Davies, Trefor Rendall, *A Book of Welsh Names*, 1952, Sheppard Press.

Drosdowski, Gunther, *Lexikon der Vornamen,* 1968, Duden.

Dunkling, Leslie, *The Guinness Book of Names,* 1974, Guinness Superlatives.

Dunkling, Leslie, *First Names First,* 1977, Dent.

Dunkling, Leslie, *What's In A Name?* 1978, Ventura.

4004 Names For Your Baby, 1972, Key Books.

Heller, Murray (ed.) *Black Names in America,* 1975, G. K. Hall.

Hergemöller, Bernd-Ulrich, *Gebräuchliche Vornamen,* 1968, Verlag Regensberg.

Janowowa, Wanda; Skarbek, Aldona; Zbijowska, Bronislawa; and Zbiniowska, Janina, *Slownik Imion,* 1975, Ossolineum. (Gives forms of names in 23 languages.)

Johnson, Charles, and Sleigh, Linwood, *The Harrap Book of Boys' and Girls' Names,* 1973, Harrap.

Kneen, J. J., *The Personal Names of the Isle of Man,* 1937, O.U.P.

Mackensen, *3876 Vornamen,* 1969, Südwest Verlag.

Mencken, H. L., *The American Language,* 4th ed. and supplements, abridged, 1963, Routledge and Kegan Paul. (Supplement: 'Proper Names in America.')

Moody, Sophy, *What Is Your Name?* 1863, rep. 1976, Gale.

Nurnberg, Maxwell, and Rosenblum, Morris, *What To Name Your Baby,* 1962, Collier Macmillan.

Otterbjörk, Roland, *Svenska Förnamn,* 1970, Esselte Studium. (Swedish)

Partridge, Eric, *Name This Child,* 3rd ed. 1951, Hamish Hamilton.

Rosenfeld, Hellmut, *Vornamenbuch,* 1968, bei Heimeran.

Seibicke, Wilfried, *Vornamen,* 1977, Gesellschaft für Deutsche Sprache.

Smith, Elsdon C., *Naming Your Baby,* 1955, Greenberg.

Swan, Helena, *Girls' Christian Names,* 1900, Swann Sonnenschein.

Stephens, Ruth, *Welsh Names for Children,* rev. ed. 1972, Y. Lolfa.

Thomson, Christine C., *Boy or Girl? Names for Every Child*, 1975, Arco Publishing.

Van Der Schaar, J., *Woordenboek Van Voornamen*, 1964, Het Spectrum. (Dutch)

Vinel, André, *Le Livre des Prénoms*, 1972, Albin Michel.

Wasserzieher, Ernst, *Hans Und Grete*, 1967, Dummlers.

Weekley, Ernest, *Jack and Jill*, 2nd ed. 1948, John Murray.

Withycombe, E. G., *The Oxford Dictionary of English Names*, 3rd ed. 1977 *Oxford University Press*.

Woulfe, Patrick, *Irish Names for Children*, rev. ed. 1974, Gill and Macmillan.

Yonge, Charlotte M., *History of Christian Names*, rev. ed. 1884, Macmillan.

The following books were also consulted:

Black, George, F., *The Surnames of Scotland*, 3rd printing 1971, The New York Public Library.

Johnston, James B., *Place-Names of Scotland*, 1934, John Murray.

Mackenzie, W. C., *Scottish Place Names*, 1931, Kegan Paul, Trench, Trubner.

Nicolaisen, W. F. H., *Scottish Place Names*, 1976, Batsford.

Room, Adrian, *Place Names of the World*, 1974, David and Charles.

Many clan names are mentioned in this book because they occur regularly as Scottish Christian names. Such names obviously have extensive historical associations. Those who wish to delve more deeply into clan history might well begin with one of the following reference works:

Adam, Frank, *The Clans, Septs and Regiments of the Scottish Highlands*, revised by Sir Thomas Innes of Learney, 1975, Johnston and Bacon.

Rennie, James Allan, *The Scottish People, Their Clans, Families and Origins*, 1960, Hutchinson.

The following list of names serves as a cross-reference to pet forms, etc., which are discussed under the main entries. For information about the first name listed, consult the article on the name that follows.

Abigail : **Gail**
Abner : **Abram**
Abraham : **Abram**
Adaidh : **Adam**
Addie : **Adam**
Addy : **Adam**
Adelaide : **Alice**
Adeliz : **Alice**
Adhamh : **Adam**
Adkin : **Adam**
Adnil : **Senga**
Adriana : **Adrian**
Adrienne : **Adrian**
Aegidius : **Giles**
Aemilia : **Emily**
Aemilius : **Emily**
Affreka : **Africa**
Affrica : **Africa**
Afreka : **Africa**
Afric : **Africa**
Aggie : **Agnes**
Aggy : **Agnes**
Agnesina : **Agnes**
Aibhilin : **Eileen**
Aidus : **Aed**
Aifric : **Africa**
Aifrice : **Africa**
Ailean : **Alan**
Aileen : **Eileen**

Ailidh : **Alice**
Ailie : **Alice, Alison, Helen**
Ailin : **Alan**
Ailis : **Alice**
Ailpein : **Alpin**
Aindrea : **Andrew**
Airchie : **Archibald**
Alain : **Alan**
Alaister : **Alasdair**
Alastair : **Alasdair**
Alaster : **Alasdair**
Alban : **Alpin**
Albertina : **Alberta**
Alec : **Alexander**
Aleck : **Alexander**
Alessandra : **Sandra**
Alex : **Alexander**
Alexa : **Alexis, Alexander**
Alexena : **Alexandra**
Alexina : **Alexandra**
Alexine : **Alexandra**
Alicia : **Alice**
Alick : **Alexander**
Alisanne : **Alison**
Alisoun : **Alison**
Alistair : **Alasdair**
Alister : **Alasdair**

Allan : **Alan**
Allana : **Alan**
Allaster : **Alasdair**
Allen : **Alan**
Allie : **Alexander, Alice, Alison**
Allistair : **Alasdair**
Allister : **Alasdair**
Ally : **Alexander, Alice, Alison**
Allyson : **Alison**
Alysanne : **Alison**
Alyso(u)n : **Alison**
Alyssa : **Sandra**
Amabel : **Amy, Mabel**
Amalghaidh : **Aulay**
Amelia : **Emily**
Amhlaibh : **Aulay**
Amhlaoibh : **Aulay**
Anabla : **Annabella**
Andie : **Alexander, Andrew**
Andra : **Andrew**
Andrean : **Andrea**
Andreana : **Andrea**
Andreas : **Andrew**
Andreena : **Andrea**
Andrena : **Andrea**
Andrene : **Andrea**

Andrewina : **Andrea**
Andrianna : **Andrea**
Andriene : **Andrea**
Andrina : **Andrea**
Andrine : **Andrea**
Andy : **Alexander,
    Andrew**
Angelina : **Angela**
Angeline : **Angela**
Angelo : **Angela**
Angie : **Angela**
Anita : **Ann**
Anleifr : **Aulay**
Anna : **Ann**
Annette : **Ann**
Annie : **Ann**
Antony : **Anthony**
Aodh : **Aed, Hugh**
Aoife : **Eva**
Aonghas : **Angus**
Aphria : **Africa**
Arch : **Archibald**
Archie : **Archibald**
Archy : **Archibald**
Arlene : **Charles**
Artair : **Arthur**
Artbran : **Arthur**
Artgal : **Arthur**
Ashley : **Melanie**
Aslaug : **Osla**
Aslog : **Osla**
Atty : **Adam**
Augustine : **Austin**
Auliffe : **Aulay**
Aumfray : **Humphrey**
Aurick : **Africa**
Avelina : **Eileen, Evelyn**
Averick : **Africa**
Avi : **Evelyn**
Avila : **Evelyn**
Averil : **Avril**
Avrille : **Avril**
Aynslie : **Ainslie**
Azile : **Senga**
Bab : **Barbara**
Babbie : **Barbara**
Babs : **Barbara**
Barabal : **Annabella**
Barbie : **Barbara**
Bartholomew : **Parlan**

Bartle : **Parlan**
Baubie : **Barbara**
Bea : **Beatrice**
Beak : **Beathag**
Beanie : **Roberta**
Beatrix : **Beatrice**
Beatty : **Beatrice**
Becky : **Rebecca**
Bee : **Beatrice**
Bel : **Isabella**
Belinda : **Linda**
Bell : **Isabella**
Bella : **Isabella**
Belle : **Isabella**
Berenice : **Veronica**
Bessie : **Elizabeth**
Beth : **Elizabeth**
Bethia : **Beathag**
Bethoc : **Beathag**
Betsy : **Elizabeth**
Bettina : **Elizabeth**
Betty : **Elizabeth**
Beverley : **Kim**
Beverly : **Kim**
Bhàtar : **Walter**
Biddy : **Bridget**
Bithiah : **Beathag**
Bob : **Robert**
Bobby : **Roberta**
Brand : **Brenda**
Breda : **Bridget**
Brice : **Bryce**
Bricius : **Bryce**
Brid(i)e : **Bridget**
Brig(h)id(e) : **Bridget**
Broder : **Broderick**
Brodhir : **Broderick**
Bror : **Broderick**
Bryan : **Brian**
Cailean : **Colin**
Caimbeul : **Campbell**
Cainnech : **Kenneth**
Cairistiona : **Christina**
Caitlin : **Catherine**
Caitriona : **Catherine**
Caoimhghin : **Kevin**
Careen : **Melanie**
Carolyn : **Caroline,
    Lynn**
Carr : **Kerr**

Carrie : **Kerry**
Cassandra : **Alexandra**
Caterina : **Catriona**
Cathaleen : **Catherine**
Catharine : **Catherine**
Cathelene : **Catherine**
Catheline : **Catherine**
Cathie : **Catherine**
Cathleen : **Catherine**
Cathy : **Catherine**
Catrina : **Catriona**
Ceanag : **Kenneth**
Ceannaideach : **Kennedy**
Cearbhall : **Carrol**
Cecelia : **Cecilia**
Cecile : **Cecilia**
Cecily : **Cecilia**
Cedrych : **Cedric**
Celia : **Cecilia**
Celia : **Sheila**
Cerdic : **Cedric**
Charity : **Grace**
Charlean : **Charles**
Charleen : **Charles**
Charlene : **Charles**
Charline : **Charles**
Charlotta : **Charlotte**
Chatty : **Charlotte**
Chris : **Christina**
Chrissie : **Christina**
Christean : **Christina**
Christeen : **Christina**
Christene : **Christina**
Christian : **Christina**
Christiana : **Christine**
Christie : **Christopher**
Christy : **Christina,
    Christopher**
Chrystal : **Christopher**
Cicely : **Cecilia**
Cinaed : **Kenneth**
Cire : **Senga**
Cissie : **Cecilia**
Clara : **Claire**
Clare : **Claire**
Claribel : **Claire**
Clarice : **Claire**
Clarinda : **Claire**
Clarissa : **Claire**
Claudia : **Gladys**

Clementine : **Clementina**
Coinneach : **Kenneth**
Colette : **Nicola**
Collette : **Nicola**
Colley : **Nicholas**
Columba : **Malcolm**
Conchobhar : **Cornelius**
Connor : **Cornelius**
Cosimo : **Cosmo**
Crisdean : **Gilchrist**
Cristal : **Christopher**
Cristinus : **Christina**
Crystie : **Christopher**
Cuddie : **Cuthbert**
Cuddy : **Cuthbert**
Cynebald : **Kim**
Cyneberg : **Kim**
Dabhaidh : **David**
Daisy : **Margaret**
Dand : **Andrew**
Dandie : **Andrew**
Dandy : **Andrew**
Danielina : **Daniel**
Danielle : **Daniel**
Davida : **David**
Davidina : **David**
Davina : **David**
Deanna : **Diana**
Debbie : **Deborah**
Debora : **Deborah**
Dederick : **Derek**
Deirdrie : **Deirdre**
Denham : **Denholm**
Denys : **Denis**
Deorsa : **George**
Dereck : **Derek**
Derick : **Derek**
Derik : **Derek**
Dermid : **Diarmid**
Dermod : **Diarmid**
Dermot : **Diarmid**
Derrick : **Derek**
Deryk : **Derek**
Detta : **Henrietta**
Diarmaid : **Diarmid**
Dianna : **Diana**
Dianne : **Diana**
Dick : **Richard**
Dickie : **Richard**
Dicky : **Richard**

Diederick : **Derek**
Dierdre : **Deirdre**
Dietrich : **Derek**
Dionysus : **Denis**
Diorbhàil : **Dorothy**
Dirk : **Derek**
Dod : **George**
Doddy : **George**
Doll(y) : **Dorothy**
Domhnall : **Daniel,**
       Donald,
       Macdonald
Dona : **Donald**
Donalda : **Donald**
Donaldina : **Donald**
Donata : **Donna**
Donatella : **Donna**
Donella : **Donna**
Donelle : **Donna**
Donetta : **Donna**
Donnchad : **Duncan**
Dora : **Dorothy**
Dorothea : **Dorothy**
Dot(ty) : **Dorothy**
Dothy : **Dorothy**
Dougal(l) : **Dugald**
Douglasina : **Douglas**
Douglass : **Douglas**
Dreena : **Andrea**
Drew : **Andrew**
Dughall : **Dugald**
Eachd(h)onn : **Eachann**
Eafric : **Africa**
Ealasaid : **Elizabeth**
Eanruig : **Henry**
Ed : **Edward**
Eddie : **Edward**
Eddy : **Edward**
Edie : **Adam**
Edom : **Adam**
Edweena : **Edwina**
Effie : **Africa,**
     Euphemia
Effric(k) : **Africa**
Egidia : **Giles**
Egidius : **Giles**
Eibhilin : **Eileen**
Eibhlin : **Eileen**
Eideard : **Edward**
Eithrig : **Africa, Erica**

Elayne : **Elaine**
El(l)enor : **Eleanor**
Eli : **Elliot**
Elias : **Elliot**
Elijah : **Elliot**
Elinor : **Eleanor**
Elisabeth : **Elizabeth**
Elise : **Elizabeth**
Eliza : **Elizabeth**
Ella : **Isabella**
Ellaine : **Elaine**
Ellenor : **Eleanor**
Ellie : **Alice,Elaine,**
     Eleanor
Ellis : **Elliot**
Elma : **Wilma**
Elmo : **Elma**
Elsbeth : **Elizabeth**
Elshie : **Elizabeth, Elsie**
Elspet : **Elizabeth**
     Elspeth
Elspie : **Elizabeth,**
     Elspeth, Elsie
Eneas : **Aeneas**
Eoghann : **Ewan, Hugh**
Eoin : **Jonathan**
Eph : **Euphemia**
Eppie : **Euphemia**
Erasmus : **Elma**
Erik : **Abram, Eric**
Erna : **Ernest**
Ernestina : **Ernest**
Essie : **Esther**
Estelle : **Stella**
Ethelinda : **Ethel**
Ethelred : **Ethel**
Etta : **Euphemia,**
     Henrietta
Euan : **Ewan**
Eubha : **Eva**
Euen : **Ewan**
Eugene : **Ewan**
Eugenie : **Bonnie**
Eugenius : **Ewen, Owen**
Euphan : **Euphemia**
Euphie : **Euphemia**
Evalyn : **Evelyn**
Eve : **Eva**
Evelina : **Evelyn**
Eveline : **Evelyn**

Evelynn(e) : **Evelyn**
Evlyn(n) : **Evelyn**
Ewen : **Ewan**
Ewhen : **Ewan**
Ezekiel : **Abram**
Faith : **Grace**
Fanny : **Euphemia,**
           Frances
Fearchar : **Farquhar**
Fearghas : **Fergus**
Findlay : **Finlay**
Finela : **Fenella**
Finella : **Fenella,**
           Flora
Finley : **Finlay**
Finola : **Fenella**
Fionnghal : **Flora,**
           Fenella
Fionnlagh : **Finlay**
Fleur : **Flora**
Flo : **Florence**
Flore : **Flora**
Florentius : **Florence**
Florie : **Flora**
Florinda : **Flora**
Florise : **Flora**
Florrie : **Flora,**
           Florence
Flossie : **Florence**
Floy : **Florence**
Foirbeis : **Forbes**
Franca : **Frances**
Francesca : **Frances**
Francina : **Frances**
Frangag : **Frances**
Frank : **Francis**
Frankie : **Frances**
Franny : **Frances**
Frazer : **Fraser**
Frederica : **Frederick**
Frederickina : **Frederick**
Freja : **Freya**
Freyja : **Freya**
Frieda : **Freda**
Frigga : **Freya**
Friseal : **Fraser**
Froja : **Freya**
Gael : **Gail**
Gale : **Gail**
Gardin : **Garden**

Gareth : **Gary**
Garioch : **Garrick**
Garret : **Gary, Gerard**
Garriock : **Garrick**
Garry : **Gary**
Garth : **Gary**
Gauvain : **Gavin**
Gavie : **Gavin**
Gawayne : **Gavin**
Gayle : **Gail**
Gellion : **Gillean**
Geordie : **George**
Georgena : **Georgina**
Georgette : **Georgina**
Georgia : **Georgina**
Georgine : **Georgina**
Gerard : **Gary**
Gerardine : **Gerard**
Gerhard : **Gerard**
Gerrard : **Gerard**
Gib(b) : **Gilbert**
Gibbie : **Gilbert**
Gibbon : **Gilbert**
Gideon : **Abram**
Gil : **Gilbert**
Gilbride : **Gilbert**
Gilean : **Gillean**
Gil(l)ian : **Gillean**
Gillandreis : **Gillanders**
Gilleabart : **Gilbert**
Gilleasbuig : **Archibald**
Gille Croisd :
           Christopher
           Gilchrist
Gilleon : **Gillean**
Gillespie : **Archibald,**
           Gillanders
Gilliane : **Gillian**
Gilzean : **Gillean**
Giorsal : **Grace**
Glyn : **Glen**
Gofraidh : **Godfrey**
Goraidh : **Godfrey**
Gordan : **Gordon**
Gorry : **Godfrey**
Graeme : **Graham**
Grahame : **Graham**
Gregory : **Gregor**
Greta : **Margaret**
Grigor : **Gregor**

Griogair : **Gregor**
Grissel(l) : **Griselda**
Grizel : **Griselda**
Grizzel : **Griselda**
Guido : **Guy**
Guy : **Guy, Gavin**
Guinevere : **Jennifer**
Gwenhwyfar : **Jennifer**
Gweniver : **Jennifer**
Gwladys : **Gladys**
Gwyllyn : **Glenn**
Hab : **Halbert**
Habbie : **Halbert**
Hadrianus : **Adrian**
Hagar : **Abram**
Hakki : **Hercules**
Hakon : **Abram,**
           Hercules
Hallbjorg : **Halbert**
Hallbjorn : **Halbert**
Hannah : **Ann**
Harailt : **Harold**
Harriet : **Harry**
Harty : **Harry**
Hattie : **Harry**
Hatty : **Harry**
Hector : **Eachann**
Helena : **Helen**
Helene : **Helen**
Helma : **Karen**
Henny : **Henrietta**
Hephzibah : **Euphemia**
Hera : **Hercules**
Heracles : **Hercules**
Hester : **Esther**
Hetty : **Esther, Henrietta**
Hew : **Hugh**
Hilarie : **Hilary**
Hillary : **Hilary**
Hob : **Halbert,**
           Robert
Hobbie : **Halbert**
Hogen : **Hercules**
Hope : **Grace**
Hosea : **Abram**
Hughina : **Hugh**
Huisdean : **Austin**
Humphray : **Humphrey**
Humphrey : **Humphrey,**
           Aulay

Hylda : **Hilda**
Ib : **Isabella**
Ibbie : **Isabella**
Ibby : **Isabella**
Ifor : **Ivor**
Ilean : **Eileen**
Ileene : **Eileen**
Ilene : **Eileen**
Inez : **Innes**
Ingeborg : **Inga**
Ingegard : **Inga**
Ingrid : **Inga**
Ingvar : **Ivor**
Iomhair : **Ivor**
Irena : **Irene**
Irmgard : **Emma**
Irmingard : **Emma**
Isa : **Isabella**
Isabel(l) : **Isabella,**
    Elizabeth
Isabelle : **Isabella**
Iseabail : **Isabella**
Ishbel : **Isabella**
Isobel(l) : **Isabella**
Isobella : **Isabella**
Isobelle : **Isabella**
Ivarr : **Ivor**
Ivey : **Ivor**
Ivie : **Ivor**
Ivy : **Ivor**
Jack : **John**
Jackaleen : **Jacqueline**
Jackalene : **Jacqueline**
Jackaline : **Jacqueline**
Jackalyn : **Jacqueline**
Jacob(us) : **Abram,**
    James
Jacobina : **Jamesina**
Jacolyn : **Jacqueline**
Jacomus : **James**
Jacqualine : **Jacqueline**
Jacquelene : **Jacqueline**
Jacquelyn : **Jacqueline**
    Lynn
Jacques : **Jacqueline**
Jaime : **James**
Jaine : **Jane**
Jamesa : **Jamesina**
Jamie : **James**
Janetta : **Janet**

Janis : **Janice**
Jannice : **Janice**
Janyce : **Janice**
Jayne : **Jane**
Jeanie : **Jean**
Jeanna : **Jean**
Jeanne : **Jean**
Jeannette : **Janet,**
    Jeanette
Jeannie : **Jean**
Jeffrey : **Geoffrey**
Jem : **James**
Jemima : **Jemima,**
    Abram
Jemmy : **James**
Jenifer : **Jennifer**
Jennie : **Janet,**
    Jennifer
Jenny : **Janet,**
    Jannifer
Jeremiah : **Abram,**
    Diarmid
Jeremy : **Diarmid**
Jess(y) : **Janet**
Jessica : **Jessie**
Jesus : **Jason**
Jill : **Gillian**
Jillian : **Gillian**
Jim(my) : **James**
Jo : **Josephine**
Jo-Ann : **Joan**
Joanna : **Joan**
Joanne : **Joan**
Jock : **John**
Jodocus : **Joyce**
Johan : **Joan**
Johann : **Joan**
Johanna : **Joan**
Johanne : **Joan**
Jon : **John**
Jonet : **Janet**
Josie : **Josephine**
Jordan : **Douglas**
Josepha : **Josephine**
Joshua : **Jason**
Josse : **Joyce**
Joy : **Joyce**
Judah : **Thomas**
Julian : **Julia**
Juliana : **Gillian**

Julienne : **Julia**
Juliet(te) : **Julia**
Julius : **Julia**
Karin : **Karen**
Katarina : **Catriona**
Kate : **Catherine**
Katey : **Catherine**
Kathaleen : **Catherine**
Kathalien : **Catherine**
Katheleen : **Catherine**
Katharine : **Catherine,**
    Karen
Katherine : **Catherine**
Kathieleen : **Catherine**
Kathleen : **Catherine**
Kathlen : **Catherine**
Kathlyn : **Catherine,**
    Lynn
Kathrine : **Catherine**
Kathryn(n) : **Catherine**
Kathy : **Catherine**
Katie : **Catherine**
Katrena : **Catriona**
Katrina : **Catriona**
Katrine : **Catriona**
Katriona : **Catriona**
Katy : **Catherine**
Kay(e) : **Catherine**
Kelly : **Tracy**
Kenna : **Kenneth**
Kennag : **Kenneth**
Kennethina : **Kenneth**
Ker : **Kerr**
Keri : **Kerry**
Kerrie : **Catherine, Kerry**
Kevan : **Kevin**
Kieran : **Kara**
Kimball : **Kim**
Kimberley : **Kim**
Kimberly : **Kim**
Kirstan : **Christina**
Kirsteen : **Christina**
Kirsten : **Christina**
Kirstie : **Christina**
Kirstine : **Christina**
Kirsty : **Christina**
Kit : **Christopher**
Kitty : **Catherine**
Kris : **Christina**
Kristin(e) : **Christina**

Kristy : **Christina**
Kym : **Kim**
Labhruinn : **Laurence**
Lachlanina : **Lachlan**
Lachlann : **Lachlan**
Lachunn : **Lachlan**
Laraine : **Laura**
Larraine : **Laura**
Larry : **Laurence**
Lars : **Laurence**
Lasse : **Laurence**
Lauraine : **Laura**
Laurana : **Laura**
Laurance : **Laurence**
Lauranne : **Laura**
Laureen : **Laura**
Laurel : **Laura**
Lauren(e) : **Laura**
Laurent : **Laurence**
Laureola : **Laura**
Lauretta : **Laura**
Laurie : **Laura,**
          Laurence
Laurina : **Laura**
Laurine : **Laura**
Lawrie : **Laurence**
Leigh : **Lee**
Lena : **Helen**
Lenore : **Eleanor**
Leonora : **Eleanor**
Lettice : **Letitia**
Lettie : **Letitia**
Letty : **Letitia**
Lewise : **Lewis**
Lexie : **Alexandra**
Lexine : **Sandra**
Liliana : **Lilian**
Lileas : **Lilian**
Lil(l)ias : **Lilian**
Lilidh : **Lillian**
Liliosa : **Lilian**
Lillibet : **Elizabeth**
Lily : **Lilian**
Lindsey : **Lindsay**
Lindy : **Linda**
Linsay : **Lindsay**
Linsey : **Lindsay**
Lisa : **Elizabeth**
Lise : **Elizabeth**
Liusaidh : **Lucy**
Lizbeth : **Elizabeth**

Lolotte : **Charlotte**
Lora : **Laura**
Loraine : **Laura**
Lorana : **Laura**
Loreen : **Laura**
Lorelle : **Laura**
Loren (a) : **Laura**
Lorene : **Laura**
Lorenz : **Laurence**
Lorenzo : **Laurence**
Loretta : **Laura**
Lori : **Laura**
Lorn : **Lorne**
Lorraine : **Laura**
Loretta : **Laura**
Lorriane : **Laura**
Lothar : **Lorraine**
Lotty : **Charlotte**
Louis : **Lewis**
Louisa : **Louise**
Lucetta : **Lucy**
Lucette : **Lucy**
Lucia : **Lucy**
Lucie(nne) : **Lucy**
Lucilla : **Lucy**
Lucille : **Lucy**
Lucinda : **Lucy**
Lucius : **Lucy**
Lucyna : **Lucy**
Ludovicus : **Ludovic**
Ludwig : **Lewis**
Luthais : **Lewis**
Lyn : **Lynn**
Lynda : **Linda**
Lyndsay(e) : **Lindsay**
Lyndsey : **Lindsay**
Lynnda : **Linda**
Lynsay : **Lindsay**
Lynsey : **Lindsay**
Mab : **Mabel**
Mabella : **Mabel**
Mabelle : **Mabel**
Maccus : **Maxwell**
Madge : **Margaret**
Mael-Moire : **Myles**
Maeve : **Mabel**
Magdalena : **Marlene**
Maggie : **Margaret**
Maili : **Molly**
Maire : **Moira**
Mairead : **Margaret**

Mairie : **Mairi**
Mairin : **Maureen**
Maisie : **Margaret**
Malai : **Molly**
Malcolmina : **Malcolm**
Male : **Molly**
Malie : **Molly**
Malinda : **Linda**
Malmhin : **Malvina**
Mamie : **Mary**
Manus : **Magnus**
Maol-Calium : **Malcolm**
Maoldomhnaich :
               Ludovic
Marc : **Mark**
Marcia : **Mark**
Marcus : **Mark**
Margarete : **Margaret**
Margaretta : **Margaret**
Margarette : **Margaret**
Margarita : **Margaret**
Marge : **Marjorie**
Margery : **Margaret**
          Maisie
Marghard : **Margaret**
Margo(t) : **Margaret**
Marguerita : **Margaret**
Marguerite : **Margaret**
Marian(ne) : **Marion**
Marieanne : **Marion**
Mariona : **Marion**
Marise : **Marisa**
Marissa : **Marisa**
Marjorie : **Margaret**
Marjory : **Margaret**
Marlena : **Marlene**
Marlyn : **Marlene**
Marrion : **Marion**
Marsail : **Maisie**
Marsali : **Margorie**
Marsha : **Mark**
Màrtainn : **Martin**
Martina : **Martin**
Martine : **Martin**
Martyn : **Martin**
Mat : **Matthew**
Mathieson : **Matthew**
Mathilda : **Matilda**
Mattie : **Martha**
Matty : **Martha**
Maud : **Matilda**

Max : **Maxwell**
Maynie : **Marion**
Meadhbh : **Mabel**
Melinda : **Linda**
Melvin : **Melville**
Melvyn : **Melville**
Meta : **Margaret**
Mhairi (e) : **Mairi**
Mhari(e) : **Mairi**
Micheil : **Michael**
Michele : **Michael**
Mich(a)ella : **Michael**
Michelle : **Michael**
Miles : **Myles**
Mima : **Jemima**
Mina : **Wilma**
Minella : **Wilma**
Minnie : **Wilma, Mary**
Mirabel, **Myra**
Miranda : **Myra**
Miriam : **Mary**
Moire : **Mary**
Moireach : **Murray**
Monro : **Munro**
Moray : **Murray**
Moreen : **Maureen**
Morna : **Malvina**
Morris : **Maurice**
Morvern : **Morven**
Morvoren : **Morven**
Morvyn : **Morven**
Morwenna : **Morven**
Moyra : **Moira**
Muire : **Mary**
Muireach : **Murdo**
Muirgheal : **Muriel**
Muirgheas : **Maurice**
Muirna : **Morna**
Murchadh : **Murdo**
Murder : **Murdo**
Murdina : **Murdo**
Murdoch : **Murdo**
Myrrha : **Myra**
Mysie : **Maisie**
Nan : **Nancy**
Nanny : **Nancy**
Nanty : **Anthony**
Neacal : **Nicholas**
Neal(e) : **Neil**
Ned(die) : **Edward**
Neddy : **Edward**

Neilena : **Neil**
Neilina : **Neil**
Neill : **Neil**
Nellie : **Helen**
Nessa : **Agnes**
Nesta : **Agnes**
Netta : **Janet**
Nevil : **Neville**
Niall : **Neil**
Nichole : **Nicola**
Nicol : **Nicholas**
Nicole : **Nicola**
Nicoletta : **Nicola**
Nicolette : **Nicola**
Niel : **Neil**
Nigel : **Neil**
Nigellus : **Neil**
Ninnidh : **Ninian**
Nita : **Janet**
Nora(h) : **Eleanor**
Noramana : **Norman**
Noreen : **Nora**
Norna : **Norma**
Nuala : **Fenella**
Nynia : **Ninian**
Obadiah : **Abram**
Odo : **Aed**
Oighrig : **Africa, Erica,**
     Euphemia
Ola : **Aulay**
Olaf : **Abram,**
     Aulay
Olav(e) : **Aulay**
Olavi : **Aulay**
Ole : **Aulay**
Oliver : **Aulay**
Olivia : **Olive**
Olle : **Aulay**
Olof : **Aulay**
Oluf : **Aulay**
Oona : **Una**
Oonagh : **Una**
Otho : **Arthur**
Ottie : **Arthur**
Otto : **Arthur**
Padair : **Patrick**
Paddy : **Patrick**
Padruig : **Patrick**
Pamphilus : **Pamela**
Para : **Patrick**
Parthalan : **Parlan**

Paruig : **Patrick**
Pat : **Patricia,**
     Patrick
Patair : **Patrick**
Patience : **Grace**
Patrice : **Patricia**
Patty : **Martha**
Paula : **Pauline**
Pauleen : **Pauline**
Paulene : **Pauline**
Paulette : **Pauline**
Peadair : **Peter**
Pearl : **Margaret**
Peggy : **Margaret**
Penelope : **Fenella**
Peta : **Peter**
Peterina : **Peter**
Petra : **Peter**
Petrina : **Peter**
Phemie : **Euphemia**
Philippa : **Philip**
Philippe : **Philip**
Phillida : **Phyllis**
Phillis : **Phyllis**
Pippa : **Philip**
Pòl : **Paul**
Quentin : **Quintin**
Quintigern : **Kentigern**
Rab : **Robert**
Rabbie : **Robert**
Rachael : **Rachel**
Rae : **Raymond**
Ragnhild(r) : **Rachel**
Ragnvald : **Roland**
Raibeart : **Robert**
Ramsey : **Ramsay**
Ranald : **Ronald**
Raoghnaild : **Rachel**
Raghnall : **Ronald**
Ray : **Raymond**
Rebekah : **Rebecca**
Regenweald : **Ronald**
Reginald : **Ronald**
Rena : **Andrea**
Reynold : **Ronald**
Rhoda : **Abram**
Ricarda : **Richard**
Richenda : **Richard**
Ringan : **Ninian**
Rita : **Margaret**
Ritchie : **Richard**

Rob : **Robert**
Robbie : **Robert**
Robyn : **Robin**
Rognvald : **Roland**
Rögnvaldr : **Ronald**
Rona : **Ronald**
Rory : **Roderick**
Rosa : **Rose**
Rosach : **Ross**
Rosaleen : **Rose**
Rosalie : **Rose**
Rosalin(a) : **Rose**
Rosalinda : **Linda**
Rosaline : **Rose**
Rosalyn(n) : **Rose**
Rosamund : **Rose**
Rosanne : **Rose**
Rosaura : **Rose**
Rosealine : **Rose**
Roseanna : **Rose**
Roseann(a) : **Rose**
Roseann(e) : **Rose**
Rosel : **Rose**
Roselane : **Rose**
Roseleen : **Rose**
Roselinda : **Rose**
Roseline : **Rose**
Roselle : **Rose**
Rosellen : **Rose**
Roselyn(n) : **Rose**
Rosetta : **Rose**
Rosette : **Rose**
Rosey : **Rose**
Rosina : **Rose**
Rosita : **Rose**
Roslyn(n) : **Rose**
Rosslyn : **Rose**
Rowland : **Roland**
Ruaidhr : **Roderick**
Ruairidh : **Roderick, Rory**
Ruaridh : **Rory**
Sadie : **Sarah**
Sally : **Sarah**
Samella : **Samantha**
Samuella : **Samantha**
Sander : **Alexander**
Sandy : **Alexander**
Sara ; **Sarah**
Saunder : **Alexander**
Sawney : **Alexander**

Sawny : **Alexander**
Scarlett : **Melanie**
Scot : **Scott**
Scotland : **Scott**
Seamus : **Hamish**
Seasaidh : **Jessie**
Selma : **Morven**
Seonad : **Shona**
Seonag : **Joan**
Seònaid : **Janet, Sheena**
Seòras : **George**
Seorsa : **George**
Sharonne : **Sharon**
Sharron : **Sharon**
Sharyn : **Sharon**
Shaun : **Sean**
Shauna : **Sean**
Shaune : **Sean**
Sheana : **Sheena**
Sheela : **Cecilia**
Sheelagh : **Sheila**
Sheelah : **Sheila**
Shena : **Sheena**
Sheenagh : **Sheena**
Sheenah : **Sheena**
Sheilagh : **Sheila**
Shelagh : **Sheila**
Shelley : **Shirley**
Sheona : **Sheena**
Shiela : **Sheila**
Shimeon : **Simon**
Shiona : **Sheena**
Shione : **Sheena**
Shonag : **Shona**
Shonagh : **Shona**
Shonah : **Shona**
Shone : **Shona**
Sib : **Isabella**
Sidney : **Sydney**
Siegward : **Shuard**
Siganhilt : **Sinnie**
Signe : **Sinnie**
Signil(la) : **Sinnie**
Signild : **Sinnie**
Sigurd : **Abram, Shuard**
Sigvard : **Shuard**
Sigvart : **Shuard**
Silas : **Sylvia**
Sile : **Cecilia, Sheila**

Sileas : **Giles, Julia**
Silis : **Giles**
Silvanus : **Sylvia**
Silvia : **Sylvia**
Sim : **Simon**
Sime : **Simon**
Simeag : **Jemima**
Simeon : **Simon**
Simmie : **Simon**
Sine : **Jane, Jean, Sheena**
Siùsaidh : **Susan**
Siver : **Shuard**
Sivert : **Shuard**
Sjur : **Shuard**
Sofia : **Sonia**
Somerled : **Samuel**
Somhairle : **Samuel**
Sonja : **Sonia**
Sonjia : **Sonia**
Sonya : **Sonia**
Sophie : **Sophia**
Sorley : **Samuel**
Steenie : **Stephen**
Stella : **Esther**
Steve : **Stephen**
Steven : **Stephen**
Stewart : **Stuart**
Stiùbart : **Stuart**
Sue : **Susan**
Sukey : **Susan**
Susanna(h) : **Susan**
Susanne : **Susan**
Suzann(e) : **Susan**
Sylvanus : **Sylvia**
Sylvester : **Sylvia**
Sym : **Simon**
Syver : **Shuard**
Syvert : **Shuard**
Tabitha : **Laura**
Tadhg : **Timothy**
Taidgh : **Timothy**
Tallaug : **Terence**
Tamar : **Abram**
Tammas : **Thomas**
Tamsin : **Thomas**
Tearlach : **Charles**
Ted(die) : **Edward**
Teddy : **Edward**
Teenie : **Christina**
Terentius : **Terence**

Terese : **Teresa**
Terkel : **Torquil**
Terrence : **Terence**
Terry : **Terence,**
    Teresa
Tetsy : **Elizabeth**
Tetty : **Elizabeth**
Thaddeus : **Timothy**
Theodorich : **Derek**
Theresa : **Teresa**
Therese : **Teresa**
Theresia : **Teresa**
Thomasa : **Thomas**
Thomasena : **Thomas**
Thomasina : **Thomas**
Thor : **Thora,**
    Torquil
Thorvald : **Turval**
Tib(bie) : **Isabella**
Tibby : **Isabella**
Tina : **Christina**
Toirdealbhach : **Terence**
Tomás : **Thomas**
Tomina : **Thomas**
Tom(my) : **Thomas**
Toni : **Antonia**
Tonia : **Antonia**
Tony : **Anthony**
Torald : **Turval**
Torcail : **Torquil**

Torcall : **Torquil**
Torkel(l) : **Torquil**
Torkild : **Torquil**
Torkjell : **Torquil**
Torlaug : **Terence**
Tormod : **Norman**
Tormond : **Norman**
Torvald : **Turval**
Totty : **Charlotte**
Tracey : **Tracy**
Trefor : **Trevor**
Tricia : **Patricia**
Trish : **Patricia**
Tristan : **Tristram**
Trix(ie) : **Beatrice**
Turlough : **Terence**
Uilleam : **William**
Uisdean : **Austin, Hugh**
Ulrick : **Kennedy**
Umfra : **Humphrey**
Umfried : **Humphrey**
Umphray : **Humphrey**
Umphrey : **Humphrey**
Unity : **Una**
Ursula : **Osla**
Valeria : **Valerie**
Valerio : **Valerie**
Valerius : **Valerie**
Vandal : **Wanda**
Vanessa : **Fiona**

Vicki(e) : **Victoria**
Vicky : **Victoria**
Vida : **David**
Vikki : **Victoria**
Vina : **David**
Vivian : **Vivien**
Vivianne : **Vivien**
Viviene : **Vivien**
Vivienne : **Vivien**
Vyvien : **Vivien**
Wardeh : **Rhoda**
Wido : **Guy**
Wilhelmina : **Wilma**
Williamena : **Wilma**
Williamina : **Wilma**
Willie : **William**
Wilson : **William**
Winifred : **Freda**
Winny : **Una**
Yehudi : **Judith**
Yiddie : **Adam**
Yngvi : **Inga**
Yve : **Yvonne**
Yvette : **Yvonne**
Zandra : **Sandra**
Zöe : **Beathag**